Building Your Real Estate & Rental Property Empire: 23+ Beginners Property Investing Strategies & Tips For Creating Wealth & Passive Income, Managing Tenants, Flipping Houses, Air BnB& More

By Unlimited Potential Publications

Table of Contents

Introduction

First off, congratulations on getting this book in your hands. There's a reason why you now have a copy of this. You have interest in investing in rental properties.

It's true that there are plenty of streams of income out there. And real estate investing is perhaps one of the best of the bunch. However, we're not talking about investing in large parcels of land or skyscrapers.

Our focus for this book are rental properties. Why this kind of property in particular? Well, think about it for a moment.

Imagine having passive income month after month. Enough to do what you want at any given time. You can invest in a new business venture, spend it on something you please, or even invest in more properties and add more cash to your bank account.

Not only that, investing in rental properties is perhaps one of the best ways to get into real estate investing itself. You'll be able to get a ground floor level look at how real estate actually works. From the buying process to fulfilling the vacancies and everything in between, you will learn exactly how to acquire rental properties that you can own and have income every month via rent payments from your tenants.

What you will learn in this book

You're going to learn a lot of valuable information. Not only will you absorb it, but you will apply what you've learned as well. Consider this book as your instruction manual to a successful career in rental property investing.

We will show you how to take certain action steps including how to form a team of trusted people that will help you become successful. And we'll also show you how to acquire your first rental property (and multiple properties as well, if you're up for it). You'll also learn a great way to acquire property using a proven system that can give you the best return on investment yet.

Not only that, you will also learn some of the ins and outs of real estate. You will learn some of the basic terminology and then some. You will also understand how financing properties work. And you will even learn how to build a robust network that consists of real estate agents, property managers, contractors, attorneys, and more.

You will also find out which courses of action are better for you. For example, are you planning on managing the property yourself or hiring a property manager to oversee it for you? Also, what kind of tenants will you want living on your properties?

This may sound like a lot of overwhelming stuff. But rest assured, learning how to invest in rental properties while making money in the process is fun to do. Sure, there are some things that you need to do that will require time, money, and effort.

But in the end, it will be worth it.

Overview of what you'll learn in this book

Cutting to the chase, here's what each chapter will cover:

Chapter 1: You will learn about the perks and joys of investing in rental property. You'll learn about how you can enjoy being an investor in such properties like single-family homes and apartment buildings among others.

Chapter 2: This chapter will show you that there are plenty of options in terms of rental properties. Whether it's residential or commercial properties, you'd be surprised what kind of properties are available for you to buy and rent out.

Chapter 3: Building your rental property empire won't take a one-man show. You're going to need to form a team of people that you can trust so you can get the ball rolling. This is an important chapter that should not be skipped.

Chapter 4: This chapter will go over the risks of investing in rental properties. Where there is reward in investing, there are a set of risks as well. If you are willing to take the risks, you can move farther along in the book.

Chapter 5: Knowing what a good rental property is takes time. And you'll soon come across one. In this chapter, you'll learn how to do some analysis and determine whether or not the properties you want will actually yield a return on investment.

Chapter 6: Once you have the know-how to analyze and run the numbers, then you can find the properties that are worth investing in. Using online and offline tools, you'll be able to find your first rental property in no time.

Chapter 7: This chapter reminds you that when it comes to finding that rental property that you want to invest in, there is always analysis that needs to be done. Learn how to properly run the numbers so you can be able to confirm that the property you want is the right one.

Chapter 8: Financing is another hurdle that you want to jump over. There are plenty of options on how you want to finance the property. This chapter will show you everything you need to know about the kind of loans that exist and how you can be guaranteed approval.

Chapter 9: This chapter will cover a proven system known as BRRRR. Once you learn the power of this system and how it can work to your advantage, it can become your go-to method for acquiring properties and getting an excellent return on investment.

Chapter 10: Your first rental property may not be in your local area. It might be hundreds of miles away or in the next state over. Either way, this chapter will show you how to expand your search area so you can find the rental property of your dreams.

Chapter 11: Are you going to manage the property yourself or have a property manager do it for you. This chapter will weigh both options so you can make the best decision.

Chapter 12: The agreement is the most important piece of paperwork for both you and the tenant. Learn what needs to be included in a rental or lease agreement and make sure that both you and your tenant come out in a win-win situation once the agreement is set in stone.

Chapter 13: Finding tenants can be a challenge. Finding the right kind of tenants can be an even greater challenge. Learn how you can screen for these tenants and put together a system that will allow you to get the right people to move into your properties while avoiding all those other bad apples.

Chapter 14: It is your responsibility to perform tasks before, during, and after a property is rented out. You'll learn how to perform walkthroughs and inspections. Also, you'll find out what you are responsible for as a property manager and what the tenant is responsible for in terms of maintenance and repairs.

Chapter 15: If you're thinking about getting out of the rental property game altogether or just building your portfolio, it's important to have an exit strategy. We'll cover four of the best exit strategies that are at your disposal.

Before we move on

A few things to go over before we move on to the first chapter. One, this isn't one of those 'get rich quick' schemes. Building your wealth with rental properties will take time, money, and effort. If you want some 'get rich quick' thing, then you're wasting your time reading this book.

Second, understand that building your rental property empire will not take one person to do it all. There are plenty of things that you need to do. But with the help of the right kind of people, you'll be in good shape (and focus on the priorities of the business).

And finally, be sure to read through this book while taking notes at the same time. There's a lot of valuable information here that just cannot be glossed over. You'll want to apply everything you've learned and jotted down in your notes.

There is no easy path to building your rental property empire. But with hard work and dedication, the rewards are oh so sweet to have. Now, let's get moving and start with Chapter 1.

Chapter 1: The Perks and Joy of Investing in Rental Property

To lead off, we're going to be talking about the perks about investing in rental properties. There is no better way to generate monthly income than someone renting your property whether it's housing or even commercial rental properties (if you want to go down that route). However, it's always good to have people who are reliable tenants that pay on time.

In this chapter, we'll talk about the perks and joys that come with investing in rental property. As the old saying goes, it's better to look before you leap. In other words, you have to know what you're getting into.

So as a word of caution, you want to read this book in its entirety before considering the idea of purchasing your first rental property. Sure, the benefits of having them are awesome. But you need to come in well-informed and have a good understanding of how it all works.

This chapter will discuss what rental property is and whether or not it can actually get you the passive income you want. We'll also talk about why it shouldn't be just a hobby and more of a business thing. We'll talk about the top four benefits along with the principles that you'll need to follow in order to maximize success.

Enough talk. We know why you're here. And we're excited that you're on board with the possibility of acquiring new property.

Let's get going:

What is Rental Property Investment?

Rental property investment is simply defined as property that is designed to get you a return on investment. Most of the time, that return on investment (ROI) will come in the form of rental income. However, another way to get a positive ROI is through the future resale of property.

However, you can get a good ROI that is generated through both means. You could have plenty of tenants sending you monthly rent every month. And when the time comes to sell, you could have more money in your pocket due to the increase in property value.

In plain English, this kind of thing is known as 'flipping'. In real estate, 'flipping' can be described as acquiring property that is sold at a low price. The reason why it may be seeling so low may be due to the low value of property and even the building being in poor condition.

Let's say that you purchase a piece of property that is a run-down and abandoned motel. You have plans on turning it into an apartment complex specifically for short-term stays (or corporate housing). You put in a good amount of money to renovate the abandoned motel and it takes you almost six months to a year to put it all together.

Now, let's say you have tenants who are professionals and executives who are in your area temporarily on business. You generate income by way of short-term leases and rent. Over time, the property value increases. After five years, you decide to sell it to another property owner who is interested in keeping the thing going.

You run off like a bandit with what might be 10 times the original investment (or a 10x ROI). That's flipping at work. And it's not just something you see on those house flipping TV shows.

Flipping will usually happen when you want to purchase property, renovate it, and sell it for more after a short period of time. Either way, the goal is getting a good return on investment. So whatever your goals are for investing in rental properties are, be sure to make a note of them.

Investment property can also be used for the purpose of holding on to it for future appreciation. Land is one of those types of property that you can invest in and it may increase in value over time for some reason or another.

What to know about investment properties

Investment properties are not used for the purpose of primary residences. These properties are designed to generate some kind of income. This income can come in the form of rents, royalties, dividends, and more.

If you intend to invest in property in the not so distant future, it's better to look before you leap (or as they say in the biz, do your due diligence). In other words, you want to do your due diligence on how to determine what may be considered the best and most profitable use of the property itself.

Will it be for single-family housing? Apartments? There are plenty of options to consider as you go.

In short, you want to figure out what would be the highest and best use of said property. Also, you want to keep in mind of the kind of property that you want to invest in. One thing to pay attention to is how the property is zoned.

If it's zoned for residential use, then your best bet is utilizing it for the purpose of living spaces such as apartments or single-family housing. Obviously, if it's zoned for commercial use, then it would be better fit for a place of business. But what if the property is zoned for both residential and commercial use?

This is where things get interesting. But it's important for you to weigh the pros and cons. What will give you the best return on investment going forward?

Once you are able to determine which approach will give you the best ROI going forward, that's when you'll use the property in that way. So if building an apartment complex for student housing yields the best ROI since it's close to a college campus, then that's when you can take the ball and run with it.

Residential vs commercial vs mixed-use: What are the differences?

There are three types of investment properties that we'll be focusing on: residential vs commercial vs mixed-use. We'll be taking a look at a comparison between the three types so you'll know the difference between them. It will also give you a basic understanding of rental properties should you invest in more of them later on down the line.

Let's take a look at the following definitions:

Residential

Residential properties are rental homes. The intent is renting out these properties for those looking for a place to live, but do not want to purchase a home of their own. You rent out a property and charge a monthly rent to tenants. These properties come in the form of single-family homes, apartments, townhomes, condos, and other residential structures such as student housing.

Commercial

Simply put, commercial properties are for places of business. While most commercial properties are not aimed to provide some kind of residential use, there are commercially owned apartment buildings. But for the most part, commercial properties are more apt to house retail businesses or the like.

Compared to residential properties, maintaining and improving these types of properties will cost more. However, because of the rent you may collect on the property on a regular basis, the impact doesn't seem all that bad. Because the leases for commercial properties will yield higher rent rates, the maintenance and improvement costs are usually off-set.

A mixed property is defined as a property that is designed for both residential and commercial use. One such example of this is the following: let's say that you own a convenience store on the lower level. On the upper level, there is a one bedroom apartment that is also part of the property.

You can collect rent for both the business and the residential property itself. Typically, it's common for a business owner to own the property in its entirety. So for you to generate income from a small business while generating rent from a tenant who lives in the apartment above you might just be a win-win.

Generate Income Passively, How True Is That?

Do rental properties generate passive income? The short answer is yes. So long as you have a positive cash flow coming from reliable tenants that pay on time, you will generate passive income from your rental properties.

What exactly is passive income? Passive income is earnings that are received from a rental property. However, you can earn it by way of a limited partnership or if you are part of an enterprise and have no active role in it.

Passive income is taxable (as it is with active income). The only difference is how the IRS handles it. Passive income is one of three main categories of income (the other two being active and portfolio). And sure enough, rental properties are one of the main examples of generating such income in the first place.

To avoid any confusion, if you decide to own land and lease it out, the income you receive from it is not considered passive. It may be more apt to quality under active income (assuming you maybe owning more land in the future). However, a landowner can benefit from the loss rules that relate to passive income if there is a net loss from the previous tax year.

Understanding cash flow with rental properties

What is cash flow? This can be defined simply by two words: income and expenses. You take the income, minus the expenses and that's your cash flow.

The goal here is to net as much positive cash flow as possible. Aside from the income and expenses, you may be setting some money aside for the purpose of renovations or the like. But if you are someone who is a buy-and-hold kind of property owner, cash flow is the best way to determine your passive income.

Why should you have positive cash flow?

Stating the obvious, cash flow is what you want. There is no sense in holding onto property that is going to lead you to losing money. So what are the reasons why you need it?

Let's take a look at a few reasons:

- **Cash flow equals opportunity:** One great example of where cash flow creates opportunity is the ability to own more rental properties. The more you own, the greater the cash flow. Sounds simple enough, right?

- **Cash flow provides a safety net:** When you have positive cash flow, it helps to have a large enough reserve for those just in case moments. And we're not just talking about repairs that may be needed. We're talking about the 'just in case' moments in your personal life like medical expenses, car repairs, and the like).

- **Cash flow gives you freedom:** Think about it. When you have cash flow of your own, it's way better than working paycheck to paycheck. Not to mention, you won't be tied down by a schedule that has you working odd hours of the day. You spend time with family, friends, and you have so much time to yourself. However, the key is to balance out that time between focusing on the properties (if needed) with your personal life. 'Work' and life doesn't have to have some imbalance.

Calculating Cash Flow

Cash flow is as follows: [Gross rental income] - [expenses and cash reserves]

So let's put this formula into action, shall we. In this example, let's say you own rental property that generates a monthly income of $1,500. Now, let's lay out the operating expenses for the month:

Operating expenses:

- **Property tax:** $200

- **Insurance:** $30

- **Mortgage:** $300

- **Property management:** $70

- **Vacancy reserves:** $25

- **Repair reserves:** $100

Total monthly expenses: $725

Cash flow: $1500 - $725 = $775

So in this example, your cash flow is $775. Not bad, right? However, let's take a look at some of the expenses up close such as the property management and reserves for vacancies and repairs.

For property management, you may want to set aside a percentage of the rental income for the expenses revolving around managing the property (such as mowing the lawn, plowing the snow in the winter, and so on). Also, set aside an amount of money that you will need to keep handy in case there are vacancies. Lastly, set a percentage of money that is needed monthly in case of repairs that need to be made as soon as possible.

What will hurt your cash flow?

There are a few factors that can play a negative role in your cash flow. It's important to know what these are so you can be able to reduce as much of the damage as possible. The following are the things you want to watch out for when tending to your cash flow:

- **Repair and maintenance expenses:** Yes, a necessary evil. Things break or deteriorate over time. As a property owner, you must be aware that these things will happen at any given time. So it would make sense to set off some money to the side each month that will cover these repairs and maintenance fees. Try not to make it too small for a percentage to the point where it can eat into your cash flow completely.

- **Tenant turnover rate:** The turnover rate for tenants will depend on various factors. The property may be falling apart or something that makes the tenant feel uncomfortable. For this reason, turnover rates can greatly reduce cash flow. Not to mention, there may be tenants who will leave without telling the property owner about what needs to be repaired. And that alone can really take a hit on your cash flow. Because of this, property managers and owners will often enact a 'new lease fee' for the new tenant to cover such costs.

- **Tenants who don't pay:** There will be times when a tenant will miss a rent payment. This could be due to financial hardship on their part. However, there may be tenants who don't even bother paying at all. If a tenant doesn't pay in full, it's detrimental to cash flow. However, those who don't pay at all means no cash flow. This means you'll have to pay extra to cover all the other expenses that you are already paying from income to begin with.

- **Property taxes and insurance:** Like repair and maintenance expenses, this is something that is a necessary evil. This is also one expense to watch closely. Your municipality or state may change the tax policy for some reason or another. Your property tax could go up or go down. In case of the former, this can hurt your cash flow. Insurance expenses can also increase at the discretion of the insurer.

- **Vacancies:** Vacancies = no cash flow. Simple as that. So it would make sense for property owners to set aside some kind of percentage of income to cover any expenses should vacancies exist. Consider it an additional insurance policy of sorts. People leaving is all part of the business. So the sooner you can fill the vacancy, the better.

How to maintain a positive cash flow

Now that you know some of the factors that can hurt cash flow, let's take a look how you can maintain it and keep it above water. These are some approaches that you should consider:

- **Increasing the rent:** Is increasing the rent a smart move? That depends. It may hurt existing tenants if you raise the rent (and can lead to them vacating). However, you can increase the rent so long as the spaces are vacant. If you want to set a rate that will be enough to generate positive cash flow, consider purchasing property that is underperforming (i.e -- if the rents are lower than the market average).

  A great way to increase the rent is by doing things that can increase the property's overall value. This includes but not limited to adding more amenities like a laundry center, air conditioning in all spaces, and more. Also, improving the property both inside and out will also help with increasing value.

- **Bring in long-term tenants:** One of the ways to ensure a positive cash flow is by having tenants stay on for the long term. Long term leases are defined as leases that last a year or more. However, you want to do your part to keep them happy and comfortable for the most part. The more you do that, the longer they will stay. One way to go about doing this is making sure that all repair needs are fulfilled in the quickest and most professional way possible. One more thing, resist the urge to increase the rent once the lease expires. It's nice to have more money in your pocket, but it's wise not to be greedy as well.

- **Consider preventative maintenance:** It's good to keep ahead of the curve when it comes to the common issues that can happen on your property. For example, take a look at your property for certain safety risks. What if there is a tree that is dangerously close to the property? A tree can fall onto a building during a storm and cause damage (not to mention any serious injuries in the process). Also, take care of things like gutters and HVAC units before they will be used frequently. Yes, there will be expenses for all of this. But better to spend now and prevent disaster than wait until it's too late (which by the way is even more costly).

- **File a property tax appeal:** As mentioned before, your municipality or state might raise property taxes. Most of the time, those increases will happen long before you even consider raising the rent. The government works fast and may usually tell no one about the increases until after the fact (unless you're keeping a close eye on things). You can appeal the property tax hike if you feel the increase itself was an unjustified move on their part.

- **Refinance the property:** This is something to consider from time to time. Conclust with the lender you are working with and see what the interests rates are for your mortgage. If they have reduced since acquiring the property, that's a great time to consider refinancing and lowering the mortgage payments. If you are successful, you increase your cash flow in the process. Win-win. But you have to double check the numbers before you make the move.

Be aware of the 1% rule

If you need to know whether or not a property will generate a positive cash flow, consider using what is known as the '1% rule'. How does this work? Let's take a look at an example:

Let's say you buy property that is priced at $150,000. The rent should be roughly $1500 a month for cash flow. As such, one percent of $150,000 is $1,500.

So, does this mean 'green light' and go? Not so fast. There are other factors and expenses that you'll need to consider.

Specifically, you'll want to pay close attention to the cost of the mortgage, property taxes, insurance, HOA dues (if such apply), and so on. Of course, you'll need to take into account what you need to set off to the side for reserves that are based on repairs and maintenance and in case there are vacancies.

Cash flow per unit

One other thing to pay attention to is the cash flow per unit. Before going any further, it's important to note that finding properties that generate positive cash flow is no easy task. Even when the market is booming, it takes time and research to find the right property to settle with.

But don't get discouraged. You'll find a piece of property that might generate cash flow and is hidden in plain sight from the other investors. In a market that isn't so hot, you will have an easier time finding a property that gives you positive cash flow.

However, the problem with acquiring properties in a 'cool market' will equal rental rates that may not be high enough to move your financial needle in the right direction. The reasons why are two things: one, there is the property value itself and the rental rates that are considered average in that location.

Not Just A Hobby

When it comes to acquiring and maintaining rental properties, some people will say it's not a fun thing to do. Others consider acquiring rental properties for generating passive income as a hobby (and get paid in the process). However, you'll want to adopt a different mindset in regards to acquiring properties.

It shouldn't really be like a hobby per se. It should be treated like a business. But still, it should be fun to do. What's not so fun about making your own money when you don't have to answer to a boss or have to work hours that you don't want to work?

So why not treat it like a hobby? Well, here are some things to consider when making the distinction between that and a business:

- Hobbies are personal. Business is professional. Repeat those two sentences over a few times. That should be one of the many mantras you might adopt in your lifetime. In business, you want to be fair and professional with your tenants. You want to keep them happy and listen to whatever suggestions or issues they may have.

- When treating it like a hobby, you become lax. So if a tenant is frequently late on payments, you give them more chances than they should. That alone can cause a lot of recoil to the point where it hurts your cash flow. Not good.

- You want to keep boundaries in place. These are boundaries that your tenants must honor. You don't want to be lax on rental payments and then turn around and put your foot down. That will cause your tenants to drive you crazy. Because of this, property managers tend to get burnt out because of the added stress that piles on.

- Treating it like a business allows you to say 'no' when you need to. You can deny a tenant based on their credit history. You can deny them based on their history as a tenant. However, don't say 'no' to them just because you can. You'll need to have a policy in place that will allow you to say 'no' for that reason.

With investment properties, you should treat it like a business. Set the boundaries and the guidelines that will help your cash flow rather than hurt it. Yes, it's fun and fulfilling to have your own business and have your own cash flow.

However, there's a balance between having fun and being professional. And it can be done without consuming too much of your time.

What if you want real estate to be a hobby?

So what if you want it to be more of a hobby rather than a business? For one, you'll want to be part of a group. More importantly, you want to be part of a group of investors that trust each other to make the right decisions and choices.

The risks of investing are smaller when it's just you and a few others in one group (as opposed to going at it solo). Someone else can handle the day-to-day operations if you choose not to do it. However, it would be incumbent upon you to relay any information and feedback from your tenants to the group if and when such a thing occurs.

Remember, you can still earn passive income even if you treat property rentals as a hobby. However, you'll still need to incorporate some solid business practices since you have partial ownership and income as part of being a group of investors. Even better, it won't be a strain on your professional and personal life.

One great way to make real estate a hobby is investing in turnkey properties. With turnkey properties, the risk of losing your investment is out of the picture and in its place is guaranteed monthly income.

Hobby or business? What should you really do?

The ball is in your court at this point. However, we can make a couple of suggestions. Rest assured, we want you to come to the conclusion that regardless if you treat real estate like a business or hobby, it still can be fun and fulfilling.

Sure, there are some downsides to this. But they are necessary evils and that's just the way things go. If you can handle the day-to-day things of managing a property, go for it.

But you'll want to build a team of people that you can trust. This includes someone who handles your legal issues, a reliable contractor that can do property management, someone who inspects the property regularly, and so on. You don't need to fill all these positions at the outset (especially when acquiring your first property).

But just know that when it comes to managing multiple properties, you'll need to work with the right kind of people in order to keep everything in line. You don't need to do everything all at once when it comes to managing your property. And you surely don't want it to be a time suck either.

While you're at it, consider connecting with your local real estate groups before acquiring property. They will be happy to help you with whatever you need before you even acquire your first piece of property. Not only will this help reduce the risk of experiencing a lot of frustrations and headaches down the road, but you'll be pacing yourself and taking your time rather than rush into something.

Top 4 Benefits You'll Get In Rental Property Investment

So what kind of benefits will you get when you invest in rental property? That's what we'll be taking a look at. Not only will you be able to enjoy financial freedom of your own, these benefits are basically just the layer on the 'awesome cake'.

Let's waste no time and jump right into what else you can get out of the whole thing:

Better asset stability

When it comes to asset stability, real estate has the best. Unlike stocks, which are volatile and can change in terms of stability hour by hour and day by day, your real estate investments are pretty much insulated from all of that.

Not to mention, you get immediate returns on your investment (namely in the form of rent income). If the demand for rental property increases, that's also the perfect opportunity to get in on the action and shore up more property and up the rent before you fulfill vacancies. From there, you'll be able to get more returns on investment that are stable and consistent.

Tax benefits

How can you say no to tax benefits? If you want to get something good back from Uncle Sam, you can with the help of rental properties. There are many tax advantages that you can get just by purchasing investment property (depending on things like how much you pay in loan interests). Not only that, you get some sweet deductions in the process that can be used to soften the blow on some expenses (like urgent repairs and the like).

More diversification

Diversification is the key word when it comes to investments. You want to spread out your investments rather than have all your eggs in one basket. With purchasing property, you can be able to diversify across many types of property.

You may already have non-real estate investments to begin with. And since they might be a little more volatile, you'll at least have something more stable like rental properties. Not only that, you won't have to worry about the value of your overall portfolio.

Real estate for the win!

Protection against inflation

Want something to hedge against inflation? Rental properties are your best bet. With inflation, the price of rent and homes goes up.

Not only that, but when inflation rises, guess what doesn't? If you said mortgage payments, you are absolutely right. Inflation and the mortgage rate are two separate things.

However, the one caveat to pay attention to is that your other expenses can rise with inflation. For example, your property tax and insurance costs can rise along with the inflation rate. If there is one figure that you really need to pay attention to, the inflation rate should be that.

So far, the inflation rate is north of a percent. And US home prices as of 2021 have risen to nearly 5.5 percent. And let's not forget, there is an increase in demand for homes (which could be a good sign if you are looking to snag up some rental properties).

Key Principles That Would Take You To Success

What are the key principles that will help you become more successful at investing in rental properties? We'll be taking a look at them here shortly. Your goal is to build and manage an empire that will create more financial freedom than you never thought was possible.

Following these key principles (without cutting corners or skipping steps) will assure you possible success. Keep in mind that the results are not usually typical compared to one rental property investor to another. Some may find success in a short amount of time while it can take longer for others.

Timing and patience are two things you'll need to have in order to succeed in building your rental property empire. With that said, here are the

following key principles to adopt so you can achieve
your own success:

It starts with effective management

In order to be successful, you'll want to do a good
job at managing your rental properties. Regardless
if you have a property manager that is taking care of
the day to day operations of one property, you are
still the manager since you own it (meaning you
have a say in terms of the property and how it
operates).

At the same time, you'll want to keep the issues of
property management at bay. You'll have
untrustworthy employees, unreliable tenants that
refuse to pay, and so much more. So you'll want to
keep those to a minimum as best you can (without
sucking the time and life out of yourself).

Remember, managing your rental properties is more
of a business. So treat it as such or you'll find
yourself drowning in a sea of negative cash flow.
Also, it helps to keep an accurate count of things so
you can be able to achieve and sustain success over
time.

Increase your income

Sounds like a no brainer thing to do, right? Increasing your income by way of rental increases or just snagging up more property (among other ways) should be something to focus on. The more you earn, the better.

However, you'll want to make sure that your property is being rented at the market rate. To set the rent price below market rate would be a mistake (and a costly one at that). So don't miss out on all that money if you are planning on setting the rent at rates that are lower than what the market averages are.

What you're missing out will add up over time. Don't be that person that is kicking themselves for missing out on that six figure payday.

Decrease expenses as well

Obviously, if you are going to increase income you might as well decrease expenses as well. There are a myriad of ways to cut expenses so you can save money. However, one thing to pay attention to is the quality of service.
And we suggest that you do not sacrifice the quality of service for the sake of saving an extra bundle of cash. It comes down to the best quality that you can afford (without killing your cash flow). So what are

some ideas and suggestions that you should consider?

Consider some of the following cost-effective ideas:

- Look for an insurer that will give you reasonable insurance rates

- If your property tax bill is too high, challenge it

- Consider installing water-saving appliances such as low-flow toilets (assuming you are paying for a water bill)

- Energy efficient appliances go a long way. If you have a laundry center on your property, consider investing in energy efficient washers and dryers

- Find a waste management company that can pick up large volumes of trash, but does fewer pickups (i.e -- Every two weeks or thereabouts)

- Place the responsibility of such expenses like utilities and the like to the tenant. It doesn't have to be a long laundry list, but something that can be manageable for their finances

Make sure you have the right people as your tenants

Screening for potential tenants will certainly be one of your best moves whenever you are managing your rental property. The bottom line is this: you want tenants who pay on time, won't cause too much of a headache, and just want to stick around for the long haul.

If you can't do the screening process, get someone who can trust. Find someone who is fair, knows the policy, and can be able to say 'no' to anyone because of what the policy states. For example, if a prospective tenant has had a history of late payments, that's a clear and resounding 'no'.

Surround yourself with people you can trust

We might have said this earlier, but will say it again. Surround yourself and choose the right people who will do a good job to keep your rental properties in good shape. This includes finding the right people who manage the property when you can't (such as collecting the rent on your behalf) and other tasks.

As your rental property portfolio grows, that's when you need to assemble the right people who will manage the property effectively and be reliable for any tasks you want done. Also, it's important to find the right people who will take care of the property and make it look good (like a property management company that mows lawns, plows driveways, etc.)

Don't get too emotionally invested

Certainly, it's a good feeling knowing that you will be able to invest in rental properties and get a nice amount of cash every month. It's a bad feeling if you tend to lose it all. Keep in mind that like most of how business works, there will be successes and failures.

When you experience some kind of failure, it's important not to get too negative about it emotionally. At the same time, there will be things that can go wrong. The last thing you want is to be stressed out about it.

Not only that, if you let your emotions get in the way, you may be making decisions that you'll soon regret down the road. Especially when those decisions show that they have a negative impact on your finances. Not only that, your tenants won't care about the work you've put into the place since you've purchased it (they care more about the byproduct of it).

Have a plan and execute it

As a real estate investor, it's always good to have a plan. To not have one is like flying blind in the fog. So it's good to have a plan for the long-term.

For example, let's say you have a goal to have a net worth of $10,000,000. How will you get there? Set the goals that will help you achieve that (both short-term and long-term).

Those goals should be reviewed on a regular basis so you know that you are on the right track. You'll know where you are at one point and be able to know where to go from there. Think of your plan like a roadmap to success.

You can't reach your goals if you don't have them set in the first place.

Final Thoughts

There are a lot of perks and benefits that go into investing in rental property. And yes, it can be fun as well. Yet, you should balance fun with business.

It can be a hobby depending on how things are structured. But we more or less recommend that you treat managing your rental properties like a business if you are serious about making money (and increasing your personal net worth). When investing in your first property, it's good to know a few things before diving in .

More importantly, know the difference between residential, commercial, and mixed use properties. If you are fairly new to the game, you should consider acquiring a residential property since they are mostly accessible to begin with. Plus, it's a lot easier to start out with for many reasons (such as the income and expenses that you need to deal with).

There are plenty of benefits to investing in rental properties. Having excellent asset stability, more diversification, a hedge against inflation, and a whole slew of tax benefits are some of the best. While there are plenty of benefits, remember that there are downsides to the whole thing.

Don't let these downsides like expenses, unreliable tenants, and the like discourage you. At the end of the day, you'll find that investing in rental properties and reaping the rewards are worth it. As long as you follow the key principles and execute on the plan you have set for yourself, you'll be in good shape for the long run.

Chapter 2: There Is More Than One Type Of Rental Property

In the previous chapter, we've talked about residential, commercial, and mixed use rental properties. As a beginner, we highly suggested starting off with residential properties because it is a lot simpler to work with compared to commercial properties (especially when it comes to dealing with expenses). In this chapter, we'll be focusing on some options that are within the residential property category.

Yes, you have plenty of opportunities all over the place. Not to mention, you could be able to acquire property and repurpose it for some kind of housing. However, it can depend on the location and even the return on investment that you'll receive in the process.

We'll be taking a look at options like single-family housing, multi-family apartments, town homes, and more. We'll also help you make the determination of which rental property will work in your favor. Each rental property does have their pros and cons (so we encourage you not to skip each section discussing a specific property).

Now, let's dive right in and see what you can be able to work with:

Options! Options! Options!

Think of the options that are at your disposal. We will be going over some of the most common residential rental property options. If you think there is a lack of them where you live, this could be due to two things: one, you may legitimately have little options to work with (possibly because you live in a small town) or you might not be looking hard enough.

There are rental properties that are hidden in plain sight. It is up to you to find them before someone else with an extra set of eyes does. Understand that with the options you have, you'll be able to know the difference between one type of property and the other.

In this chapter, you will know the difference between single-family housing and perhaps student housing. There are different types of rental housing such as assisted living facilities, halfway houses, income-based housing, and so on. However, these options below are some of our best recommendations.

Let's begin by taking an even closer look at single-family rental houses and how they can work to your advantage.

Single-Family Rental House

Just so we're clear, your first residential rental property doesn't have to be an apartment building. You can start off with one single tenant if you're more comfortable with it. However, this will most likely require a single-family house that is under your ownership.

A single-family rental property will be a house that you rent out to someone who may be living alone or may be living with a significant other (with or without kids). Also, there could also be a few people living together as roommates and want a bigger space compared to an apartment.

Like this and the other types of property will be looking at, we'll be going over the pros and cons of each. Single-family rental homes may be your cup of tea or it something else might be. Are single-family homes right for you?

Let's find out by laying out these pros and cons:

Pros of single-family housing

- **Longer leases:** One of the main goals for any rental property owner is having a tenant who can stay for the long-term. Long-term is anywhere from 12 months and beyond. So it makes sense considering that you can have a tenant who is reliable and pays on time for the long term. And longer leases equals a better ROI (be it monthly or annually).

- **Lower property taxes:** In the previous chapter, we suggested that you should consider keeping expenses reasonably low. With single-family homes, you pay less in property taxes compared to different types of property like apartment buildings. On top of that, commercial real estate is taxed differently compared to real estate that is zoned for residential use.

- **Lower management costs:** Keeping in continuation with minimizing expenses, a single-family home. When it comes to these types of property, the repair and maintenance costs will be relatively low. Once again, the expenses are not that bad compared to apartment buildings and the like.

- **Resale value can improve:** Let's say you have a tenant that is leaving because they purchased a home of their own. At the same time, you're thinking about selling the house to someone as well. You can sell the house for more than what you bought for it in the first place. The resale value will increase under the condition that the house is in a neighborhood that is thriving. Also, if the property is kept up well, the resale value could be even better. Your tenant may have put in some work or you might have some work put in before you consider selling it yourself.

Cons of single-family housing

- **HOA fees:** Payable HOA fees can be a damper on a rental property. This means you will need to pay some kind of monthly fee. This may be due to the amenities that are available in the neighborhood. If you want to avoid these kinds of fees, ask around the neighborhood where your target rental property regarding if an HOA exists.

- **Land size:** If you are looking to rent out a single-family home, there may be tenants who may decline the offer because of the land size. They might want more land (or perhaps an even larger backyard for the kids). That doesn't mean you can own a house that has a large amount of land as well. Sometimes, you win some and lose some because of the amount of acreage.

- **Vacancies mean lower ROI:** When a tenant vacates, that could mean a temporary decrease on your ROI (assuming you hold more than one piece of property). Once the lease agreement ends, the tenant can choose to renew or not. Keep in mind that when it comes to finding a new tenant, increased costs aimed towards fulfilling a vacancy will arise.

- **Initial sale price may be higher:** When buying a house for the purpose of renting it out, you may contend with higher prices. That's because the house itself can be renovated for the purpose of increasing the value. On one end, someone is focused on increasing the resale value (while the other is facing the necessary evil of having to buy it at a higher price). That happens all the time in real estate. But it is what it is.

For those who are renting a single-family house, there's a reason why they are going this route. Maybe they're holding off on buying a house in the future. They might need a large amount of space like a garage or an attic. Whatever the need, there is a good chance they'd be willing to pay rent for it as opposed to purchasing it outright.

Multifamily Apartment

A multifamily apartment is a residential property that contains more than one unit of housing. These include but are not limited to duplexes, townhomes, apartments, condos. With multi family homes, you can be able to generate a good ROI since you'll likely be renting these out to multiple residents.

In other words, one family can live in a downstairs apartment while another family lives in the apartment above. If you are looking to purchase a multi-family home as a primary residence, you are welcome to do so. From there, you can rent a vacant space to a family or someone looking for a living space.

This is what is known as owner-occupied properties. Regardless of how you approach multi-family apartments and housing, it's a great rental property to invest in. So what are the pros and cons of this property type?

Let's take a look at them:

Pros of multifamily apartments

- **Better cash flow:** Of course, you have a better cash flow (not to mention an even large amount of it) when you rent multifamily apartments. You could stand to make double the rent from two people renting separate spaces (one renting the downstairs, the other the upstairs at let's say $750 a month for each tenant)

- **Increased valuation potential:** Multifamily real estate does appreciate in value. At the same time, they can hold their own when things don't look so well in terms of the economy. While there really is no timetable on when you'll see an increase in value, they are bound to happen at one point in time or another

- **Keeps insurance simple:** Did you know that the insurance policy for apartment buildings can be a bit more complex? So if you are not one to wrestle with all of that, but want to rent out multiple units, then multifamily apartments may be your best bet. Not to mention, once you acquire more multifamily properties, they can all be simply covered under the same insurance policy. Plus, you deal with no further complications at all

- **Tax benefits:** Obviously, the recurring pattern for these rental properties are the tax benefits. So what will you get from renting out multi family properties? Your mortgage payments and the interest you pay on them may yield some tax benefits in the long run. You may also qualify for some pretty cool deductions as well.

Cons of multifamily apartments

- **Cost:** Yes, the cost for a multifamily apartment is going to be high compared to single-family housing. At the same time, you'll need to consider the location that you are in. The closer you are to a major metropolitan area, the more expensive it will become. If you are starting out and find multifamily units appealing, consider going a bit farther away from the city center

- **Management can be complex:** When dealing with multiple family properties, the juggling can get a little complete. There are tenants who have different expenses from the other. Some of them have different repair and maintenance needs. So keeping track of these things can be difficult at times. You can find a way to organize these and handle them on your own or have a property manager handle some of the operations to take the weight off of things.

- **They are a bit more competitive:** When it comes to investing in properties, you will run into some competition. The more appealing the property, the more competitive it can get. Multi Family homes are typically one of the most competitive properties out there. Why? For one, they are not dealing with so many units. So the costs will be less compared to an apartment building. On top of that, going at it along on your first try is going to be difficult. So it would be smart to team up with people who have experience in investing in this kind of property.

- **Regulations:** Depending on the kind of property you are investing and managing in, there's a good chance that you may run into some kind of regulations. The regulations set upon multi family homes are way different than single-family homes. Not to mention, those regulations may be stricter compared to the latter. That's why it is important to team up with someone who may be experienced (such as being part of a group investment). These experienced investors have been there and are aware of the laws and regulations that may be in place.

On the surface, multifamily properties will more than likely give you a nice boost in ROI. However, for the newbie, handling the common downsides that comes with it all can be a bit overwhelming. If you have never owned rental property, you'd be wise to steer clear from multi family homes until you have some experience under your belt.

Alternatively, you could become part of an investor group. But the entry to get in may not be easy. For now, put multifamily units on the backburner until you have a clear understanding of what you are getting into.

Student Housing

Student housing might be a great option for first-time investors like yourself. College students may be getting tired of the dorm life. So they may opt for some larger space.

Most student housing complexes will fare well in larger universities (think schools with a large student population of 10,000 or more). These major universities will have a mix of dorms and student housing for upperclassmen, graduate students, or even law or medical students. In college sports terms (assuming you are a fan), Division I schools are a good place to start.

So there are opportunities in student housing. And it can be perfect for a first-time rental property that you can invest in. We'll outline some of the pros and cons with student housing right now:

Pros of Student Housing

- **It's fully managed:** Not only will you have someone managing the property, but there will always be someone on site who can be able to check on the property regularly for any repairs, maintenance, and the like. Plus, there will likely be a maintenance crew on site (employed by the University or a similar entity).

- **The demand is always strong:** Think about it. There are students who come and go from schools. One class graduates and a new one enters. So the demand for student housing will remain strong so long as people are going to school. Of course, there will be options that students will have in terms of housing. The dorms may be good, but there's always the option for larger space if a dorm room isn't enough.

- **Amenities are usually available:** Even if you purchase the property, odds are there will be nearby amenities. So you don't have to provide them for yourself (unless there is a demand for them). Students won't mind the regular commute from their apartments to a place nearby.

- **Long-term tenants:** With student housing, you'll usually have tenants that will stick around for the long-term (i.e -- the duration of their schooling). Of course, one tenant will leave and another will soon fulfill the vacancy. So you won't have to worry about vacancies staying empty for long.

- **Multiple income streams:** Depending on how much per unit is, you'll have more streams of income for each apartment. Some may be the same price while some larger spaces will yield a higher rent. The more units that are occupied, the better.

Cons of Student Housing

- **No year-round tenants:** While there are long-term tenants, the caveat is that they won't be in these apartments year-round. Some of them will be returning home during the summer break. However, one way to remedy that situation is to offer summer housing for those who are taking short-term summer classes (or those who may be taking on internships in the local area).

- **Competition is solid:** Certainly, there is solid competition in the student housing market. While private developers are building their own complexes, the universities themselves might be doing the same.

- **There may be additional 'hoops':** There are some extra hoops that you may need to jump through depending on your jurisdiction. This may include extra licenses and regulations. This may be considered a necessary evil rather than something that discourages you from investing in student housing.

- **The lack of credit history:** Students may come into college with little to no credit history whatsoever. For landlords and property managers, they rely on credit history to determine whether or not a potential tenant has the financial stability. Couple that with the potential of what limited income they may have and it may be a risk that you may be willing to take.

- **Repairs and maintenance is likely:** We're not saying that all students love to get rowdy and make noise. However, there will usually be some parties going on. And people might just have a good time and forget about the surroundings. So things might get broken to the point where it might be a busy week for the repair crew. Consider setting off a percentage of money for repair and maintenance expenses.

Student housing presents you with some pretty good upsides. Yet, the downsides still exist. It's not as complicated of a property to invest in because you already have the management team already on staff (most of them will be employed and paid for by the school). Plus, there may be nearby amenities that are a quick skip and a hop away.

Finally, there's a steady stream of tenants who may be looking for off-campus housing. Dorm life may not be something that some students would want anyhow. So they'll need a place to live that is close to the campus, but doesn't include a ton of noise at 2AM.

Town Homes

Town homes (or known by alternative names like townhouses or a row house) is a multistory property that will share one wall with a property that is adjacent to them. Townhouses have their own private entrance, driveway, garage, basement, and backyard. One thing to keep in mind is that in neighborhoods where there are town homes, there is usually an HOA attached to it.

So what are the pros and cons of town homes as a rental property? Let's have a look:

Pros of town homes:

- **You have your own tenants**: Whether it's one or more town homes that you are renting out, there's a tenant for each one. It's not like you are renting out apartment units. So it's similar to renting out a single-family home (except it's a little different with town homes). With one town home, you own the exterior and the interior of the property.

- **Maintenance is fairly easy**: If there is an HOA on the property, they will take care of the maintenance on their end. So long as you pay the maintenance fees every month, that is. A majority of the maintenance will be covered, but sometimes you may need to cover it yourself. Regardless, consider saving up on repair and maintenance reserves just in case.

- **Lower costs**: The cost of investing in a town home is actually lower than you think. They are even lower in price compared to single-family homes. If you are someone who is looking to invest in rental property, but might be looking for a cost-effective option, chances are you can consider town homes as the best investment to start out with.

- **Modern design:** Townhomes mostly have modern designs compared to single-family homes. Designs that are modern and look brand new will more than likely attract more tenants compared to something that's been built decades ago. An attractive design and a great price might just be the two best things that your tenants may be looking for.

- **Excellent rental income:** Of course, rental income potential is what you're looking for. Town homes provide you with a great opportunity to snag a good amount of it. Town homes are usually popular with families that want a good amount of space. Not to mention, they are quite affordable in terms of rent (when compared to apartments, condos, etc.)

Cons of town homes:

- **Extra fees:** Town homes will usually be attached to an HOA. This means that HOA fees will probably be an expense that you need to account for every month. Also, there are maintenance fees that will also get factored in (even though a majority of the maintenance is handled by the HOA).

- **Limited use:** In town home neighborhoods, the uses may be limited. The reason why is that there may be rules and regulations in place by the HOA. While there are town homes in one area that can be rented out, you may not have them rented out in the way you intended. So it's better to consult with the HOA first before making an investment in town homes.

- **Acquiring an investment loan can be difficult:** In terms of financing for town homes, it may be a challenge to acquire a loan. The banks have the final say on whether or not you'll get a loan. Usually this is due to the fact that compared to single-family homes, town homes are much more modern. And banks are hesitant on whether or not they should issue loans.

- **Privacy issues with tenants may arise:** Since town homes will likely share a wall with an adjacent town home, this can put off potential tenants. Especially the ones who place a high standard on privacy. You can come and go as you please, but don't count on not being watched by your neighbors.

- **Noise issues:** Since you are sharing a wall with the people next door, there's a good chance that you'll be hearing noises from their end (and vice versa). Potential tenants may be turned off by that considering that they need their peace and quiet for a good chunk of the day.

- **Space may be limited:** The space for town homes may be limited. Specifically, we're talking about storage space. Sure, you'll have a garage and a basement for all of that. But how much storage would you need for all the Christmas decorations and the like? Also, the living space may be a little cramped (or even a bit too cramped for anyone's liking)

Other Rental Properties To Consider

Now that we have covered some of the most common rental properties that you can invest in, we're not finished yet. There are other rental properties to invest in if you are not too keen on the idea of investing in one of the property types above. So what else is there to consider?

We'll be looking at three different types of property to invest: properties known as ' fixer-uppers', foreclosures, and of course commercial real estate. There are a set of pros and cons for each (which will take a look at so you know what to expect). In the meantime, let's start with fixer-uppers:

What are 'fixer-uppers'?

To simply put it into plain English, fixer uppers are properties that are not in the best of conditions. They are in need of repairs that may very well be major repairs at best. This could include replacing entire systems such as plumbing and renovating the entire home from the ground up.

If you got the extra cash to make repairs even after purchasing the property itself, then you might find a fixer-upper to be something that will be worth your while. After putting in the work by way of repairs and renovations, you'll see your hard work pay off in the form of your ROI. Certainly, it will take time to see an ROI because you will be spending time fixing the place up (hence the name).

What are the pros and cons? Let's have a look:

Pros of Fixer-Uppers:

- **Purchase prices are lower:** With properties that are in need of repair, the purchase prices will be much lower than those that are in good shape. No two houses are priced equally. The good news is that the house will have a low barrier for entry if it needs a lot of repairing. Fixer-uppers tend to go for prices under the average market value. Expect prices to be at least 8 to 10 percent below the average as a good starting point.

- **You control where the money goes:** Clearly, you'll be investing in plenty of money towards repairs. So you get to make the decision of where that money will go. Do you want to put money towards fixing the entire HVAC system? Go for it. Does it need any kind of renovations in the kitchen or bathroom? That's for you to decide. After purchasing the property, take a look around and make a list of repairs and renovations that you feel are worth the investment. The most urgent or highly prioritized repairs and renovations should be the first thing you focus on before anything else. For example, if the foundation or the structure is showing signs of wear and deterioration, focus on that first.

- **Competition is lesser:** If you are looking for investment property where there is less competition, then fixer-uppers are your best bet. That's because your competitors may not even bother with the idea of putting in an additional investment that goes towards repairs and renovations. The mindset for most of your competitors will be 'quick and fast gains' with as little work as possible. So they hate putting in more risk than they think is necessary.

- **An opportunity to increase value:** Think about it for a moment. If you put in plenty of work, then odds are you will increase the value of your property over time. So what are you waiting for? A single-family home that looked horrendous from the inside and out will gain plenty of value so long as you put in the work (no matter how long it takes). How much of an increase are you willing to aim for? That's up to you.

- **Forced appreciation:** When it comes to the overall value of your home, the only direction for a fixer-upper to go is up. Simple as that. It won't depreciate in value farther than it has to. Even if you add plenty of value to it, you can be able to sell the property at a higher price if you want to (or flip it). However, you intend on generating passive income out of the whole thing. So perhaps setting the rent price will be more sufficient.

Cons of Fixer-Uppers:

- **Additional money is needed:** Even though you purchase the home below the average market value, that's just one of the lower hurdles to jump through. Now, the real challenge begins with needing additional money for the repairs and renovations needed. Once again, it's a necessary evil that is required for adding more overall value to the home. Not only that, you could be looking at hidden expenses based on unexpected repairs that may seem to pop up as the process moves along.

- **You may go over your budget:** You might already have a set budget in mind for renovating and repairing your fixer-upper. Yet, there's a good chance that you may go over that budget. 40 percent of rental property investors stay within the budget (but still, there's a chance that you may go over for some reason or another). Again, this can be connected to expenses that are unplanned or suddenly appear. You may discover some no so pleasant things like asbestos or even rotting beams.

- **An uncertain future:** The timeline for turning a fixer-upper into a home that looks great for someone to move into will usually be inconclusive. That's because you'll be dealing with some surprise discoveries, the repair process, and so on. So it would be wise not to make an estimate on how long it can take. Just focus on the repairs and know that the end result will be in sight sooner rather than never.

Foreclosures

Another investment property that has a low barrier of entry is foreclosure properties. The prices are below the market value like fixer-uppers. But still, there are risks that do exist.

Structural wise, they should be fine (unless there are some repairs needed). The problems that may lay ahead include the financial side of the property. We're talking liens, unpaid taxes, and similar issues.

While foreclosures are a good investment, you may want to do a little deep diving on the target property before making a splash. It's a good thing we have a set of pros and cons to help you out. So let's have a look at what to expect (including the common downsides):

Pros of Foreclosures

- **Discounted value:** The good news about foreclosures is that they will come at a discounted value. So if you want a lower barrier of entry on the financial front, this kind of property will be perfect for you. The even better news, there are low to no down payments (depending on the financial institution that you are going through).

- **A great ROI opportunity:** If you are looking for a great ROI opportunity, chances are a foreclosure property may be just what you're looking for. Granted, it won't take a long time to get a positive ROI because of the lesser need to make repairs. You can be able to get a tenant into the home quickly after the home is inspected and passes.

- **Closing process is fast:** If you want to snag the property and waste as little time as possible, then foreclosures will be your best property to focus on. The closing process is much quicker compared to purchasing the home going through the regular process. On average, it takes 30 days to close on a foreclosure. The length of time if it was just any regular house? Almost double the time (60 days).

- **You may not see or inspect the home:** There's a good chance that you as a property investor may not be able to see or inspect the home before making a decision. Almost every foreclosure on the market will be sold on an 'as-is' basis. So you'll mostly get what you get no matter what.

- **They may be fixer-uppers:** Nobody likes surprises. When purchasing a foreclosure and you see it for the first time, you'll notice it's more of a fixer-upper than anything. So think of purchasing foreclosures like a wrapped gift. You'll never know what's inside (or outside) until you tear off the paper. So the likelihood of putting in an additional amount for repairs and renovations is good. You might as well set off some extra money to the side in case such an obligation should be fulfilled.

- **Slightly more competitive than fixer-uppers:** Because of the mystery surrounding foreclosures, there are investors that want to get in on the action. They want to know what they are working with. For this reason, you'll be seeing some additional eyes (other than yours) watching the property and have their intent to purchase. Inventory can go quicker than it can be fulfilled. So stay one step ahead of your competitors and pay attention to auctions that focus on foreclosures.

Commercial Properties

Early on, we mentioned commercial properties as one other investment property to consider. However, this might be something that a beginner should refrain from focusing on until they have a bit of experience under their belt. But, if you do have plenty of money aside to invest in commercial properties, then it may be wise to know what to expect.

Here are the pros and cons that you'll need to be aware of regarding commercial properties:

Pros of Commercial Properties

- **Higher ROI:** Yes, the rents will be higher than residential investment properties. So right off the bat, you get a much higher return on investment. If you are looking to get a substantial gain, then a commercial property could be what you're looking for.

- **Leases are longer:** While long-term residential leases are basically 12 months or longer, the commercial leases are even lengthier. On average, a long-term commercial lease will range from three to five years. This will at least help you secure some long-term tenants. Who may be considered reliable in the long-term? Consider larger companies and corporations, well-known brands, or even the government (or a specific department).

- **Great for diversification:** As mentioned earlier on, investing is great when you are diversifying your assets. So if you have residential properties, you may feel inclined to invest in a commercial property. Residential properties here and commercial properties there? No problem. As long as you're getting a solid ROI on it, what harm can it do?

Cons of Commercial Properties

- **Vacancies can be lengthy:** When it comes to vacancies, it may be quite lengthy for a commercial property compared to residential properties. While you can be able to fulfill the residential properties much faster, it can take as little as six months to find the right tenant for your commercial vacancies. For this reason, it's important to set aside some cash just in case that happens.

- **Lease terms are complex:** With commercial leases, there are some complexities that exist. This may include some legal help on your end to help draw up a lease of some kind.

- **Upfront capital needed:** When purchasing commercial property, there is upfront money that will be needed to acquire the property. And that amount of money might be a lot. The amount of money needed will depend on the type of commercial property that you intend to purchase.

How Do You Choose?

Now, the million dollar question is this: Of the properties that we have listed above, how will you choose between one or the other. It's important to consider a number of factors before making a final decision.

At this point, you may have a good idea of which property you may be investing in. But what if you are still undecided? Let's take a look at some considerations that you'll want to mull over before making what could be the most important decision of your life (so far):

How much money will you have on hand?

The financial end of any deal should always be taken into consideration before anything else. How much money do you think you'll need? No one knows for sure until they do some research and come up with some estimates.

If you don't want to spend a ridiculous amount of money on properties, then you could settle for something like a fixer-upper or a foreclosure property. So long as you know what you're getting into or don't mind paying a low price for the initial property (and adding more money for repairs and such), these are the properties that you can spend money and time on.

If you are looking to acquire other properties, the base number you'll want to start with is the amount you're willing to spend on a certain rental property. So if there's a single-family home that you want to purchase that has a $100,000 price tag, then that's the base number to start off with.

How much work are you willing to put in?

If you are looking for rental property that will require less to no work, then you may look at different investments such as single-family homes, apartments, or even student housing (among others). These are the properties that you want to focus on if you are simply looking for a quick gain in ROI. Remember, these types of properties will be competitive, so you better come in with a solid strategy in mind.

However, if you don't mind putting in the extra work for the purpose of increasing the properties value and getting a much greater ROI in the process, once again focus on the properties that will give you less of a headache in terms of entry (i.e -- foreclosures or fixer-uppers). If competition is something that you don't want to deal with, fixer-uppers may be your best option in the long run.

What kind of ROI are you looking for?

For most rental property investors, they are looking for something quick, easy, and large in terms of ROI. While it might sound like a tempting thing to do, there are some downsides that you will need to contend with. For example, commercial properties will more than likely yield the greatest ROI compared to residential properties.

However, as a beginner you want to start off small and build from the ground up. Unless you have the cash to buy a commercial property (and cover initial expenses), any kind of residential property would be a good starting point in terms of a modest ROI. You can rent out a single-family residence or a townhome.

To start out with a base ROI and moving your way up would be a smart thing to do. That's because you'll deal with less hurdles and headaches like expenses and having to put in all kinds of work trying to find the right tenant.

What property gives you long-term tenants faster?

Aside from a solid ROI, one major goal a property owner must fulfill is finding a tenant who can stay on for the long-term (12 months or more). On paper, commercial properties will likely be the best option since the leases tend to be lengthier than residential ones. However, if you want to stay within the residential side of things, your best options are single-family homes, multi-family properties and townhomes.

Student housing will yield some long-term tenants, but with some caveats. They won't be around for at least a total of three months out of the year. So if you are looking for long-term, year-round tenants then the aforementioned properties in this section will be what you need to focus on.

Simpler lease terms

Easy choice in this regard would be residential properties. The lease terms won't be that complicated. All you have to do is lay them out with little to no legal consultation as possible (only needed when there may be an issue).

The terms will be more complex when dealing with commercial properties. If you don't want to deal with all kinds of legal headaches throughout the process, residential properties might be right up your alley.

Final Thoughts

Now that you know that there are plenty of options for rental properties, you know that opportunities are pretty much everywhere. The choices may seem a bit overwhelming at first. However, you'll be able to make a process of elimination based on your needs and what you don't want to deal with in terms of obstacles.

That's why you should spend as much time as possible making the determination of which property will work best in your favor. Yes, it can take some time. But you'll feel that once you've made the right decision, it was worth the investment in time to look at the right kind of property that will give you a better ROI.

The world of rental properties is looking better than ever. While there are many options to look at, you'll want to pay attention to the barriers of entry and even the competition that exists within each type of property. Our advice is to take the road less traveled if you are a complete beginner.

In other words, find a property that will give you less competition (like fixer-uppers). Bear in mind though, you might want to be aware of the other obstacles that stand in the way (like repair costs and the like). Rental properties are great whenever you want a good overall ROI. Sometimes, it may take some work to get there.

But nevertheless, you have an opportunity to start building your rental property portfolio. With time and more money in your pocket, you will still be able to build your portfolio with a mix of properties that you might like. You may have a lot of residential properties with some commercial buildings mixed in.

It pays to find the right kind of property. So determine what benefits you want out of the whole thing and consider which obstacles and barriers that you want to avoid.

Chapter 3 - Meet Your Team Members

One thing you need to understand is that investing in rental properties will be hard to do when it's one person running the show. This is going to take quite a bit of work to do. Not to mention, you'll want as many eyes and ears on the ground as you can.

That's why it is important to have team members in your corner helping you find the best property that will give you an excellent ROI. In this chapter, we'll discuss why forming a team is important. You will learn the kind of roles that each team member will play and why they are essential to your success.

We may be tempted to go at things alone. However, there are some things that will take quite a bit of time. So doing a lot of time-consuming stuff by yourself will definitely take a lot out of your day. You may feel discouraged at first thinking that finding a rental property is easy.

However, the process is a bit more complicated than you think. But as long as you surround yourself with the right kind of people, you might be in a good position to snag the property you want to rent out and get a nice slice of the pie.

Now, let's dive right in and discuss why it will take more than one person to help you succeed at investing in real estate and the kind of people you want to find so you can leverage their expertise and strengths.

Let's get right to it:

There's No 'I' in Rental Property

It would be a mistake to tackle the great big world of real estate all by yourself. Especially when there are a lot of financial and legal things that are usually involved. Not to mention, you'll be working with people who want to be your tenants. And it would be your responsibility to keep them happy so they can stay on your property for the long-term.

Instead of saying 'I' in terms of rental property, adopt the following as your mantra: 'Team work makes the dream work'. Repeat it over and over again either in your head or aloud. This group of people should be people you trust and rely on for their expertise.

When it comes to success, it is always important to surround yourself with the right kind of people. Early on, we discussed that you should connect with local real estate groups on social media. These are people who know their stuff and will probably be happy to lend you a hand as a new investor.

If you haven't made the connections yet, now would be a good time to do so. You'll want a base network to help you build your team from the ground up. People know people who have a certain skill or talent that you are looking for.

Important People That You Should Include In Your Team

So who should be on your team? What kind of tasks are you looking to fulfill? This section will help you find the kind of people that you want to hire for a certain task and why.

Remember, there are some moving parts to the whole process of acquiring a rental property. And you certainly don't want to do everything. Let's take a look at the kind of people you'll need and why they are essential to your team:

Seekers

These are your realtors and 'property scouts'. These people are your eyes on the ground whenever you are in the hunt for rental property that has excellent

ROI potential. You want people that know the local market like the back of their hand.

These are the people who have vital information about the local housing market. They know which areas are valuable and which ones that may be on the up and up. If you are looking for someone who has access to a list of properties that you can acquire and rent out, you want a seeker on your team.

As a reward, they can become one of your investing partners (and they too can have a slice of the pie). At the same time, they may be looking to build out their own rental portfolio as well. With their success in helping you find a property, they can be paid a finder's fee (which can be a percentage of your total ROI).

Lenders

Odds are that you may need to take out a loan that can be used for acquiring target properties. So it's good to have someone who is a lender on your team. These are the people who will loan you cash so you can be able to acquire the property you want.

On top of that, a lender that you can trust can also be someone who can open the door of new opportunities for you. One thing to look for is whether or not if a lender will provide you with some flexibility. You'll also be introduced to the wide variety of loans that are available.

These include but are not limited to fixed portfolio loans (available in 5-year or 10-year terms), 30-year fixed single asset loans, or acquisition lines of credit for those looking to fix and flip homes. The loans you'll want will depend on what your plans are for the property that you acquire.

Tax professionals

When it comes to taxes, you'll want a couple of important people on your team. This includes a certified public accountant or CPA. The other is a tax attorney.

A CPA will be someone who will keep track of your finances. Meanwhile, your tax attorney will be there to help you through the legal process in terms of paying taxes (and even giving you assistance whenever you want to challenge your tax bill or the like). An experienced attorney will know plenty about the tax code and will assist you in establishing a plan that can be executed in the event of something such as incapacitation or death.

Property managers

If you want people to manage properties for you (because you can't be everywhere at once), find someone who can do it. This can be one person or a management company. Self-managing might be something that you can try your hand at.

But unless you want calls at 3AM about something being broken or the toilet not flushing properly, a property manager will definitely be a worthy addition to your team. A property manager will also play a role in who will be able to occupy vacancies as a tenant and who may be denied due to policies that are in place.

Insurance agent

Let's face it: things happen. Disaster can occur at any point in time whether it's rain or shine. So it would make a lot of sense knowing that you have an insurance agent in your corner.

Especially someone who can give you an excellent insurance policy that will cover things such as severe property damage and the like. You'll want things like business liability, property protection, and some other essentials so that you are covered for the unexpected (whenever those things occur).

Not only that, but having an insurance agent in your corner may also give you the opportunity to snag a good policy at a reasonable price. When looking for insurance agents, see if you are able to find out how much each policy is worth. Remember, you don't want to start out with a large amount of expenses (nor do you want to skimp on some kind of coverage just for the sake of saving money).

Title company

Need someone in your corner to help you close the deal much faster? That's where title companies come in. They will help you determine the final evaluation of the property you want to acquire.

A title company will give you access to people who can do research on what you are actually looking to acquire. You might get a glance at the repair history so you know the kind of condition it's in. And you'll also learn about the kind of insurance coverage it has received in the past.

They will help gather the right data and information that will help make closing the deal a lot easier (or if you feel that you may be walking into a bad deal that could cost you).

Contractors

Having the right contractors on speed dial will put you a step ahead of so many rental property owners.

There will come a time when repairs and renovations may be necessary. So you'll want to find the right team that will focus on any vital repairs needed such as the structural integrity, what systems can be installed like plumbing and HVAC, and even those who are experts at installing kitchen sets and the like.

Appraisers

Lastly, you want someone who has a good eye and knowledge of what valuable property looks like. You want someone who can give you an estimated value of the property before setting rent prices or even selling the property altogether when the time comes. Appraisers will give you the most accurate assessment possible.

Find an appraiser who has experience working with investors. Especially when it's someone who can give you a good estimate while the property is vacant. From there, you can either do one of three things: fulfill the vacancy with a new tenant, make some repairs to increase the value, or sell it outright.

Where to find your dream team

Though we mentioned it a bit earlier, finding your dream team may be closer than you think. For one, you should find out what real estate groups are in your local area. The ability to network with people who know a thing or two about real estate (and work with other investors) will help you get your foot in the door.

It's always important to leverage your network. The power of who you know will help you in the long run. Someone may know someone who is a mortgage broker.

Another person may know a CPA and a tax attorney that you can work with. There are real estate professionals out there that can help a new investor like yourself connect with the right kind of people. So where can you find these networks of people?

Here are a few ideas to keep in mind:

- **Social media groups:** You'd be surprised how many real estate experts you can find on social media these days. Especially in places like Facebook or LinkedIn groups. It wouldn't hurt to find a real estate group that focuses on your local area. Add yourself to these groups (if they are available). Find the right people who you think are worth connecting with. Also, don't be afraid to ask questions for the purpose of just picking their brains or getting a feel of the local market.

- **Networking events:** There has to be a lot of industries that put on networking events throughout the year. If there is a networking event that is focused on real estate and close to your local area, why not attend it? Meeting real estate experts face to face may be a little better than say meeting them online. Especially when it's hard to read a person on social media. You can attend seminars and learn of a few ideas of what may be going on in the world of real estate.

- **Check the real estate database:** Somewhere on the Interwebs (and beyond), there's a list of real estate experts that you can connect with. And it can be as simple as a Google search to gather the information on who the realtors are in your area. These are people who may work with investors in helping you buy your first property. And while they're at it, they may also recommend people who will become a part of your team along the way. Once again, don't be afraid to ask around so you can assemble the right kind of people.

- **Home and trade shows:** In-person events are great (as we have mentioned before). What better way to connect with those who know a thing or two about real estate than home and trade shows. You can strike up a conversation with people who do residential contracting and get a good idea of what their expertise is. You may also run into real estate agents who may have some property to take off their hands (so you can rent them out for your tenants).

There are so many opportunities at your disposal. Especially when you want to build your team from scratch. When you're starting out, you can choose one person as a point of contact and build out your network from there. Remember, this takes time and effort among all things.

The important thing for you to do is to not overwhelm yourself and focus on one thing at a time. Keep it as simple as you can get it. Plus, you can always refer to this book as a reference whenever you get stuck with something.

Final Thoughts

When you are building your rental properties empire, you should never go at this alone. There are plenty of things that need to be done in order to achieve the success you want. It's great to have extra sets of eyes and hands on the ground.

More important, you want to connect yourself with people who you can trust. These are people who will help you succeed in any way possible. Whoever you choose as part of your team must be knowledgeable, competent, and professional.

You know where to find them. And you can reach out to them at any time (or during business hours). However, you'll want to be respectful of their time.

Therefore, if you are planning on asking some questions or do some fact-finding about investing in rental properties, you can reach out to your people of interest. Ask them to speak to them for about 10 or 15 minutes at best. That way, they can give you enough time before moving forward with the rest of the day.

Keep in mind that aside from time and effort, you'll need good communication skills, a willingness to give something back in return, and nurturing your network for the long run. Don't expect a lot if you are not giving anything back in return or communicating with your team members once in a while.

When fielding through a list of people for certain roles, it's important to ask yourself some questions. Are they professional? Have they been helpful in one way or another?

Remember, these are the people who you will be dealing with for the long-term. So you better have a team that is professional, helpful, and willing to communicate with you regularly. When the team cultivates a relationship with each other, success can be closer than ever.

With the right kind of property manager, insurance agents, tax advisors, and other team members at your side, you can be able to build your rental property empire from the ground up. It takes a dream to make the dream. And be sure to give credit to those who have helped you along the way.

Chapter 4: Are You Willing To Take The Risk?

The one word that you will always hear no matter what you invest in is risk. It doesn't matter if it's property, stocks, bonds, or even cryptocurrency. There are risks that are usually taken when there is money involved.

You can lose it or make gains. The percentages will vary depending on various factors. But at its core, investing is putting a risk into something and possibly getting a return out of it.

Do not confuse investing with gambling (although carelessly spending or investing money in something without the due diligence may very well be gambling itself). It's important to know what you are getting into before you put any kind of money down. In this chapter, we'll be talking about risk (and whether or not you'll be willing to take them).

Investing isn't an easy thing to do. You can win some, but you will lose some. That's the nature of the business.

But don't let the idea of risk or potential loss discourage you. We'll talk about the common reasons why rental property owners fail (and thus risk losing their initial investment in the process). After the end of this chapter, you'll realize that taking risks in investing rental properties may not be all that bad.

Let's get right to it:

Risks Are Everywhere

Just like investment opportunities, risks are everywhere. Sure, you'll want to be aware of the returns that you get from putting down the initial amount of money. But you have to understand the risks that are involved as well.

There are some obvious risks that you'll need to look for before you decide to spend your hard earned money. That's why doing your due diligence is so important. Risks can depend on the performance of some factors like the economy.

What else could also be affected? Let's take a look:

- **Political change:** It doesn't matter your beliefs or if you care for politics or not. But political change can affect your real estate investment as a whole. Specifically, one such issue to pay close attention to is property taxes. Will they go up or down? Will there be any regulations that may hurt your investment in the long run?

- **Technology changes:** As you're reading this, we are living in an age where technology changes can have some kind of effect on a person's property. For example, the way we consume energy. People may be switching to solar panels to save up on energy costs. New technology can phase out the old and make way for the new. Thus, it creates uncertainty for your investment.

- **Consumer confidence:** If there is one barometer to determine whether or not investing in something is worth the risk, it's the market itself. The consumer confidence in a product, service, or even property will yield some kind of positive or negative feedback. And that feedback can generate more business or slow it down (to the point where almost no one wants to spend their money on it anymore). This is one more reason why you should keep your tenants happy while they are renting from you.

- **Company risk:** You may be part of a group and someone who holds a major stake in the partnership decides to cash out and call it good. This may happen unexpectedly and without prior knowledge given to the rest of the group. Their financial position might be even greater than their initial investment and they decide that cashing out and moving on would be a good move on their part. As for the rest of the group, what could that mean for the investment itself?

Unearthing hidden risks

While there are risks that appear on the surface, there are those that are located beneath it. So what exactly are they? Here's a brief list of those risks so you know what they are and why they can affect your investment:

- **Inflation:** Yes, inflation happens. And it can cause profits to go down as prices rise. For this reason, you'll see interest rates tumble (which can cause your overall investment to take a hit). The purchasing power that you may have once had may weaken.

- **Interest rates:** As mentioned before, interest rates are a hidden risk within themselves. These rates will rise as bond prices do in a downward trajectory. In a time when the economy is going strong, there will be a higher demand for money. And for that reason, you'll see interest rates go up. Could a good economy equal a better return on your investment? It's possible.

- **Liquidity or illiquidity:** So what's the difference between these two? Liquidity is the ability to convert something into cash without hurting the overall value of the investment. Meanwhile, illiquidity will force you to sell any investments even at a low price (so your return may not be the best). Also, you may not see your investment reach full maturity.

- **Currency fluctuation:** What kind of role does currency fluctuation play a role in? Are we talking about the valuation of the dollar? Or are we talking about the exchange rates between the US dollar vs other currencies (such as the Canadian Dollar, Euro, etc.)?

What Are The Risks?

Already, we've taken a look at some of the risks of general investing on the surface (and what's underneath it). So what are the risks of property investment? We'll be taking a look at them here shortly.

As someone who is fairly new to the idea of investing in rental property, you may need to know the specific risks that happen. So you'll want to know what they are so you can be more successful at choosing the right kind of property. Let's take a look at the risks that pertain to rental properties:

Vacancies

Vacancies occur for various reasons. One can happen when a tenant finds a better place to live (or purchases a home of their own). Another would be because of how poorly managed the property may be.

So it's important to reduce the number of vacancies on your property as much as possible. As we've stated before, vacancies equal a reduced income to no income at all (depending on the type of property you invest or own). Beyond the vacancy itself, there's usually the repairs and maintenance that can happen if the outgoing tenant left the place in worse shape than it was before.

This means having to dip into your cash reserves and the like to cover the repair and maintenance costs. Depending on the severity of the damage and how long the repairs take, that vacancy may not be filled for quite awhile. Otherwise, you'll want to find a new tenant as soon as possible.

Decrease in rent

One of the times when rent rates decrease would be when the economy is going in a downward direction. Clearly, a lot of people may not afford the rent because of lost wages and the like. And this means you may need to reduce the rent itself. When people lose money, so might you.

Not only that, you won't be the only rental property investor or owner dealing with this. You'll also have other investors lower their rental prices to stoke the flames of competition. And this can lead you to lowering the rent on your own terms.
So in an economic downturn, you could expect price wars brewing between rental property investors. And you might be in the thick of it all. And that is why it's more of a risk rather than a good move.

There's a difference between being forced to reduce the rent compared to reducing it to where you can get a tenant to fulfill the vacancy. The former will pose an even greater risk. So pay close attention to how things are going economically if you want to stay ahead of the curve.

Decrease in property value

Like the decrease in rent, the property value can decrease and thus present the possibility of losing a bit of money from your initial investment. When the property value decreases, that means selling at a lower price when the time comes.

What causes property value to decrease? There are a handful of factors. For one, the property itself may be in need of repair or renovation.

So it would be your responsibility to make those repairs or renovations when needed. However, the property value may decrease due to things that are beyond your control. This can be due to environmental factors or something that may affect property values throughout the entire area to drop altogether.

It can take a single 'eyesore' that is adjacent to your property to affect your value as it is. You can do something about it in a few ways. It could mean consulting with your local government or banks (assuming they may have control over any abandoned buildings that may be near your property).

Bad tenants

If you are just allowing people to become tenants without screening them properly, this can cause a ton of problems. For example, you could have tenants that will be lax in payment. You may also have people who can get rowdy and break things (which means more money going out the window due to repair expenses).

This is one huge reason why you'll want a property manager to handle all the tenant-related matters (including who gets to move in and who doesn't). There needs to be certain policies in place to ensure that you get the right kind of tenants (while warding off the low quality ones).

Bad credit scores, history of missed payments, or even a criminal record could be some strikes against tenants looking to move into a place located on your property. A bad tenant or two can trigger so many headaches. So choose wisely.

Operating at a loss (or negative cash flow)

If you are operating at a loss or have a negative cash flow, this can cause your investment to lose its value. That's why you want to operate at a positive cash flow so you have a positive return on investment. Operating at a loss on a temporary basis may be fine, just as long as you find a long-term solution in the process.

For example, let's say that one of your expenses increases. A property management company decides to increase their rates and it puts your cash flow slightly in the red. At that point, you can do one of two things: one, you can increase fees or the rent. Two, you can find a cost effective solution by finding a property management company that can get the job done at a lesser price.

In this situation, you may be faced with a decision that could impact the tenants. If you do have some vacancies, consider upping the rent before it's filled. The rent of your existing tenants should remain the same to ensure that they stay happy and are not surprised by any hikes.

Conditions of the market economy

The market economy is one of the major things that every real estate investor must pay attention to. Especially if you are going to focus on building your portfolio of rental properties. The market economy will play a role in the rental property's future value.

This is what affects your rental income, the resale value, and the like. So if you are contemplating the idea of purchasing property (or cashing out), see what the state of the market economy is like. If it's in good shape, by all means have at it.

The deeper you understand the market, the more you'll be able to make a few moves ahead of your competition. You'll be playing chess while the others may be playing checkers. And that alone could put you on top compared to those who have been in the game for quite some time.

What Makes Rental Property Investment Challenging

As a rental property investor, you may be aware of the challenges that lie ahead. But what are those specific challenges? This section will lay that all out for you.

Those who are willing to take on the risks and challenges of rental property investing can find success for the long-term once they stick with the plan and be able to conquer the challenges that are set before them. If you don't know how to overcome the challenges, you'll learn how right here.
These are the challenges that entail with investing in rental properties (and how to rise above them):

Financing

The first major challenge that you'll face as a rental property investor will always be the financial side of things. You may have a handful of cash to spend on a property that you've had your eye on. But the issue here is that it may not be enough to cover the purchase itself.

So it seems that the best route for most investors is applying for a loan. You may have $50,000 on hand, but need an extra $50,000 to purchase a $100,000 property. There may be a few lenders that can get you the cash you need.

You want to take a look at some of the terms, conditions, and policies that will ensure your approval. If you don't meet them, you will be denied (even right off the bat). As a property owner, one of your expenses will be the mortgage (or repaying that loan back to the lender).

The one thing that will help you rise above financial challenges is making sure that you have a positive cash flow. Yes, it can be solved with rent income (but let's not forget the expenses that go along with it). Speaking of which, let's move on to the next challenge.

Fulfilling the vacancy

Once you have purchased the property you want, the question that you must ask is: who will fulfill the vacancies? This means searching for the right kind of tenants that will stick around for the long-term. Who will be willing to sign a 12 month lease for an apartment or a single-family home?

A good tenant is usually hard to find (as strange as it sounds). You'll have some that will miss payments. You'll have one or two of them who can get rowdy and make noise.

The truth is, you'll need to set some policies and guidelines as to who will be able to become tenants of your property (and who can't). Before you even fulfill such vacancies, determine whether or not you want to do this yourself or have a property manager do it for you.

Knowing whether to renovate or not

Renovations can and will happen at some point. The question is: how long will it be until it finally happens? Whether it's small-scale improvements or something greater, you may consider renovations to be something of a positive rather than a negative.
One such thing that a renovation may yield is a higher return on investment (and even higher rents). Finding the right time to renovate may seem like a difficult task. The no-brainer option would be when there is a vacancy.

What if there are renovations needed when there are tenants currently occupying the unit? This is for you and the tenant to discuss. You can talk about what needs to be done and perhaps work out some kind of deal with them.

If it means the tenant possibly paying more, consider what they would be willing to have in order to justify paying a higher rent. You want both you and the tenant to come out of the deal with the two of you on the winning side.

Unreliable tenants

Of course, you'll have tenants that won't pay. Or they won't keep the place in good condition. The place may be damaged to the point where the handyman is there every day (and might as well be an additional tenant).

Before laying out your battle plan on how to deal with unreliable tenants such as evicting them, it's good to brush up on the tenancy laws in your jurisdiction. Also, you'll want to review the terms of the lease. Your tenant has rights and obligations and you want to honor them as such (and avoid legal headaches).

This is where a professional property manager will come in handy. When you are assembling your team, this property management (or management company) can handle all the heavy lifting regarding unreliable tenants so you don't have to.

Not making enough money

This is a challenge that will likely happen in the beginning. And it may happen in situations where there are more vacancies than there are occupants. This is one of the largest challenges that a rental property investor faces regularly.

The two options to handle this challenge can't be simple enough: one, you cut down expenses or you increase the rent. With vacancies, increasing the rent may be easy to do. But what if you have existing tenants?

You may have tenants that will not be happy with the rent increase. And that could mean a turnover. So it would be wise to speak with them and let them know about your consideration before making a major move.

Is it possible to raise the rent while retaining the tenant? The short answer is yes. However, the tenant may not be the only person you'll want to consult with.

This is something that you'll want to discuss with your property manager. You want to raise the rent, but how much would be a reasonable hike? On top of that, are there any legal things of note to look into before making the move?

This could be a challenge that you will face if not enough money is being made. But thankfully, you have options to ensure that your cash flow stays in the green.

Top 3 Reasons Why Rental Property Owners Fail

When it comes to investing in rental properties, there is the possibility that someone will fail. We'll be taking a look at the top three reasons why. You want to learn which mistakes to avoid so you can be able to have a more prosperous future as a property investor instead of a bleak one.

These are the reasons:

1. Risking too much

As the old saying goes, big risk equals big reward. And for some investors, their greed can kill their chances of getting a good return on investment. They can do that by betting on a huge risk.

Overleveraging or obtaining deals that may be considered 'low-down' deals (or those that never have materialized) are just prime examples of taking risks. The more risks you are taking, the more than likely you'll be hearing the words 'bankruptcy' sooner rather than later.

No matter how hard you try to avoid it, there will be some risks. And no investment is considered 'too safe'. But if you are able to navigate it with ease, you'll stand to lose less as opposed to more.

2. Lack of education

If you know too little about investing, you'll lose quite a lot of money on 'this investment or that investment'. One of the reasons why you are reading this book is because you want to learn how to invest in a specific asset. Needless to say, you're in the right direction.

Even after you finish reading this book, the education continues. So it's important to learn the right things in order to achieve success with investing in rental properties. You'll want to build an educational foundation that will support your future success.

The best ways to acquire this education is by doing your research. And it also means connecting with people who have been dealing with real estate for quite some time. It also never hurts to have people who have rental properties in their portfolio as well.

Oh...and steer clear from those sleazy late night infomercials that promise that you'll get rich quick with real estate. Those are not real educational materials (and really not worth the money).

3. You are not doing any due diligence or analysis

With every investment, there's one thing that you absolutely must do. And that is do your due diligence and analysis. When you first start out, you might think you know what you're doing.

But the reality is, you might be doing something wrong and not know it until it's too late. In your analysis, you must be careful. You must study the numbers and see if there is a trend going in the right or wrong direction.

No, you cannot predict the future. But you can use your best judgement while analyzing things and determine whether or not it's worth the investment. And best of all, you better make sure that the math is right and on point.

You can simply avoid failure by not making the mistakes listed above. Be sure that you're not taking too much of a risk. And you'll want to learn a good amount about what you can regarding rental properties.

And as always, for the love of everything that is right in this world, look before you leap. In other words, do your research and analyze any available data. If the math appears to be off, then that might be a hidden signal to hold off on making an investment (or move on to a property that will yield a better return).

It is Not as Scary as it Seems

Even though there are risks, that should not discourage you in the slightest. Remember, it should be fun and exciting to get into the world of investing in rental properties. But you have to know your limits.

All it takes is good planning, relying on the right information, and being able to analyze and relevant data that will help get you on the path towards prosperity. It may also be a challenge to distinguish which information is considered the real deal from the stuff that may be false and full of empty promises.

Remember, finding success will take trial and error. Do you have what it takes to take the risks while making sure you stay within your limits? We hope so.

Final Thoughts

Indeed there are risks that take place whenever you are investing in rental property. It's about making sure that you understand the risks and finding ways to rise to the challenge so you don't end up losing your shirt. It's all about looking at the bigger picture and the long-term rather than look at investing as an opportunity to 'get rich quick'.

It's important that you find the right people and the right information so you know what you're getting into. If you make one bad investment due to some misinformation, that's one thing. But doing it repeatedly for one purpose or another may be asking for trouble.

Investing in rental property isn't for everyone. Those who are not willing to take some risks should refrain from it. Those who cannot embrace failure should consider something else.

And those who don't feel like putting in a lot of work and analysis should consider investing in rental properties. It may not be easy to do, but the rewards certainly are sweet.

Chapter 5 - Knowing What A Good Rental Property Is

There is a rental property that is waiting to be bought by someone who is willing to take good care of it. Not to mention, it's an opportunity that just might be hidden in plain sight. It might take a good set of eyes to spot it when everyone else is overlooking it.

For the investor that has spent a good deal of time generating rental income, they seem to miss opportunities that are considered to be hidden gems. In this chapter, you'll learn some of the ins and outs of knowing what qualifies as good rental property. Sure, you may find something that will be appealing enough to purchase (but there's always something better).

We'll also dive deep and discuss how you can find a good rental property with the help of a few different resources (including one that a lot of people don't seem to utilize all that much). You'll also learn about things like the price to rent ratio so it will help you generate a good amount of income in the long run.

Let's move on and talk about the choices that you might face when selecting your first rental property:

There's A Good Choice and a Better One

There will come a time when you'll come across a rental property that has some good quality features. You might be in a good neighborhood and the property itself is in good shape. You have the money to snag it today if you wanted to.

However, one of your 'eyes on the ground' spots something that might be a little better. And yet, there are some qualities about the property that might just make it more valuable in the future.

Good neighborhood? Check.

Commute-friendly? Check.

Close to the city center? Double check.

Location is one of the most important aspects of acquiring a good piece of property. However, you'll want to take into account the numbers. That's why analysis is so important.

Being able to crunch the numbers and examine them after words will help you make a choice on which property is the best. Sometimes, no matter how good it looks or how close it is to points of interest, the numbers will usually tell you otherwise.

What are some of the calculations to keep in mind while taking a look at the properties that interest you? Let's take a look at the following:

Return on investment (ROI)

Obviously, you want a good ROI. At the end of the day, the property that tends to have the highest overall ROI will win out. Remember, the overall ROI will be calculated by the following formula:

(Net profit/Cost of the investment) x 100

The percentage or ratio should be in the positive. After crunching and calculating the numbers, if it is positive, that's when you know that you'll be making a profit. Obviously, a negative percentage or ratio will equate to a loss (sounds simple enough, right?).

Net Operating Income

The net operating income is the amount of profit that is generated on an annual basis from an investment. You calculate this using the following formula:

Net income - net operating costs
Remember, the operating costs include your expenses such as taxes, maintenance, supplies,

insurance, and so on. You might already have a few set expenses in mind. So be sure to calculate those whenever you are putting together the numbers.

Also, keep in mind that the expenses on one property will be manageable while it may not be the case on another property for some reason or another. Also, know that the older the investment, the more the operating costs will be.

Cash on cash return

This is defined as how much the cash ratio will be for the investor. The calculation for this will be useful for investors that want to finance their property investment with long-term debt. For this reason, investors won't be too focused on the operation costs.
The return itself will give them an indicator of how good the property is performing.

Capitalization rate

The cap rate is calculated as follows:

(Net operating income/Property value in the current market) x 100

Before you even snag the property that you're interested in, you must always look at the property value in the current market. Remember, there's a good chance that the market can change for the better or the worse (depending on economy and other factors). If the current market is looking solid, then the property values shouldn't be too shabby.

Bear in mind that if you invest in the property and get the same amount of money from it while the market gets better, the cap rate will drop. Obviously, you'll see the opposite happen if the market drops (albeit sharply).

The cap rate should be something you'll want to calculate with each property you are looking at. It does change from one property of interest to the next. The lower the rate, the better.

Rent Ratio

The rent ratio is the monthly income to the cost of the property. This is how you calculate it:

[Total annual rent/total cost of the property]

The ratio you want to aim for is higher than one percent. If the ratio is lower, then the investor will need more time to recover the total cost of the property itself. For example, let's say the rent per month was $1500 a month and the total cost of the property was $150,000.

Take the total amount of rent you pay annually (so in this case, $1,500 x 12 is $18,000). Now, let's calculate the rest of it to get the rent ratio:

[$18,000/$200,000 = 1.2]

So the ratio is just above a percent. But you get the idea. Sometimes, it may take a bit more time to recover the total cost of the property based on the rent you are charging per month because of a low ratio.

The Demand Is High But The Vacancy Is Low

Aside from the analysis of data, you'll also want to take into consideration the following things: the demand and the vacancy rate. The vacancy rate is determined as follows:

[Number of days vacant / number of rentable days]

For example, if there was a property that was vacant for 30 days, the rate would be the following:

30 / 365 = 8.2 percent

If you have a portfolio property of say 3 homes, here's how you calculate it:

Total Vacant days/Total rentable days (365 x # of properties) = Rate

Let's say for vacant days, Home #1 has 30, Home #2 has 21, and Home #3 has 14. In total, you have 65 vacant days. You multiple 365 by the number of properties you own. So in this case, you multiple 365 by three.

Let's finish up the formula:

65 / 1095 (365 x 3) = 5.9 percent

Then you have the occupancy rate that is calculated like using the following formula:

[Rentable days - vacant days]

So, in this case you have 30 vacant days. Minus that by 365 and you get 335 days that the property was occupied. Now, let's calculate that number to get the occupancy rate:

335/365 = 91.7

So the occupancy rate for this example is 91.7 percent.

Why are all these numbers relevant? For one, a low vacancy rate will equal a high demand. If the rate is below 2 percent, the rental demand will be high. If the rate is higher than 4 percent, the market will signify that there is plenty of supply to go around.

If there is a low vacancy rate on your property, your property manager will have plenty of applicants to field through. Many will apply, but not everyone will be approved as a tenant. Not to mention, with the demand being high and a low vacancy it's prime for the potential of upping the rent before the vacancy itself is fulfilled.

On top of that, the low vacancy data means that the competition will be a little less cluttered. There will be a pool of available tenants but you might have a good chunk of them applying to fulfill the leftover vacancies you may have.

One takeaway from this: if the vacancy rate is low, you and the property manager have to be selective when it comes to who will move into your rental property. So that may come down to a few tough decisions. Use your gut instinct if you need to.

Employment Opportunities Matter

Job growth and the housing market go hand in hand. Not only that, the latter is one of the biggest components of the US economy. Remember when the housing market crashed in the late 2000s?

Yep, for that reason the economy took a major hit from it. This further supports the statement that you want to check for how the rest of the economy is doing before diving in. That's why doing your due diligence is so important.

Naturally, the housing market will fare well when the job growth is positive. When the job growth goes in the opposite direction, the housing market will take a hit (and a lot of people may not be so keen with buying a house at that moment). Also, the likelihood of fulfilling rental vacancies may not be as good.

There is an issue where there is high unemployment rates and high vacancy rates. This puts property investors in a precarious position.

The job market and the unemployment rate will play a huge factor in your investments. Let's take a look at a few things that you'll want to be aware of:

- When the unemployment rate is high, your property value will take a hit. Likewise, the number of tenants will be lower since they may not desire looking to fulfill a vacancy somewhere

- If the unemployment situation is worse enough, the likelihood of property foreclosure will be even greater. If your property is located near other properties that are foreclosed (or in the process of doing so), that will drag down the value of your own property.

- If the employment rate is high and people are working, the demand will be steady. However, if the vacancy rate is high, you may want to consider reducing the rental rate so the vacancies get fulfilled.

When you are looking at vacancies to fulfill, the job growth is a key indicator. If the unemployment rate is at a low level, consider reducing rent to a point where it can be a reasonable amount for your ideal tenant. If the unemployment rate is high, be prepared to make some financially tough decisions.

If you have enough money lying around, you could consider acquiring some of the adjacent properties that have been foreclosed. However, you might risk putting yourself in a position that you'll have more unfilled supply with low demand. So it might be best just to bite the bullet and deal with a lower property value.

One thing to keep in mind is that job growth forecasts can play a role in rental prices. If there is future job growth predicted, that could give you enough time to choose which properties you want to up the rent for. Be sure to take a look at how the wages and total household income numbers are moving.

The Neighborhood is a Key Player

If there is one indicator that will help you make the determination of whether or not you are making the right choice in terms of property investment, the neighborhood is your best friend. You could ask people living in the neighborhood about certain types of information like the nearest schools, average commute time, safety, and so on.

Using that intel will help you get an inside track on whether or not the target property is actually worth investing in. Think about it for a moment: a family of four would want to rent a single-family home. However, they have some wishes and needs in where they want to live.

For example, they want to be near a school. They also want to be in a neighborhood that is safe and has a low crime rate. And they want to at least have a short commute to work at best.

Can you blame someone who wants all those things? No. And that's why you'll want some neighborhood information from the people that know it best: those who live there.

On top of all of this, you'll want to do some number crunching. While scouting the neighborhood, take a look at the number of houses that are currently up for sale. You'll want to get the exact addresses of these homes so you can get data on them (such as the asking price).

Also, the number of owner-occupied homes will help you determine whether or not if the houses up for sale are worth renting or if it's just for purchasing only.

Lastly, the vacancy and occupancy rate is key. Ask people living in the neighborhood how long they've lived there. The higher the occupancy rate, the lower the vacancy rate.

Average Rents and Average Property Value

One more number to focus on when looking for property to invest in is the price to rent ratio. This is calculated with the following formula:

[Median Home Price/Median Annual Rent]

If the median home price in one neighborhood of interest is $200,000 and if you plan on renting out a place at $1,000 a month, this is what you need to calculate:

$200,000 / $12,000 ($1,000 x 12 months) = 16.6

The price to rent ratio can be used to determine the potential demand for rental property in the area. The higher the price to rent ratio, the higher the demand.

Final Thoughts

At this point, you may be thinking about choosing a rental property that will be perfect for your portfolio. However, this will require you to do plenty of number crunching and analysis. Using the simple formulas we've listed above, the number crunching won't be too difficult.

However, it's better to get an understanding of how the numbers operate. They will be used to determine demand and whether or not the property you are looking at may actually be worth it. Some other property may come along and end up being better (not because of the location, but the numbers will tell you otherwise).

The vacancy ratio will determine a demand for rental properties (as will the price to rent ratio). Also, keep in mind that the economy and the job market will play a role in your decision. A good time to jump on an opportunity is when the job market is doing good. If the employment rate is high but the vacancy rate is high as well, then you've got plenty of supply that can be fulfilled.

It also doesn't hurt to get some information by going straight to the source, the people who live in the neighborhood you are interested in. The more you know about the neighborhood in general, the more likely you can consider snagging a rental property there.

Chapter 6 - Rental Properties and Where To Find Them

Now, here comes the fun part. Now it's time to find some rental properties that you might like. In this chapter, we're going to be taking a look at multiple approaches.

One thing you need to understand is that you shouldn't be stressed out too much about looking for a rental property. You may be asking yourself, 'where can I find a property'. Rest assured, this chapter will serve as a good starting point and help put your mind at ease.

There are plenty of valuable tools to use that will help you find the right kind of properties. Not to mention, you'll be able to determine whether or not if there is a good solid demand for such properties or if there is a supply just waiting to be fulfilled. Even in today's technology driven world, you'll find some prospective acquisitions to look at and put together a list of multiple properties by the end of the day.

You'll be learning about how to use a heatmap (and how they work). You'll also learn about the MLS (or multiple list services) along with an old-fashioned tool that has helped rental property investors like you in the past and still works today.

With that said, let's jump right in. This is one chapter that you really shouldn't skip for obvious reasons.

Finding Properties Are Easier Than You Think

We're in the 21st century. So it comes as no surprise that our current technology can be harnessed for a greater good. In this case, you'll be using it for the purpose of finding your rental properties. As mentioned earlier, we'll be taking a look at some tools of interest that will work to your advantage.

With the help of modern day technology, it takes off a lot of pressure and stress that happens when trying to find the right kind of property. We encourage you to use these tools often so you can be able to determine whether or not the property you are eyeing is actually worth it. Let's move forward and talk about heatmaps.

Heatmap Is A Great Tool To Start With

A heatmap might just be one of the coolest tools for any rental property investor to use. It is an analysis tool that can also serve as an investment tool as well. A heatmap uses color codes to determine hot and cold spots.

The hot spots will usually be darker in color ranging from yellow to red. Meanwhile, the cool spots will be yellowish-green to about green or blue (depending on what the indicator lists). You'll be using this tool to find out which areas have excellent property values, demand for such property, or even any kind of data that may be relevant to a target area.

You can find a real estate heat map anywhere online. There are plenty of different websites that have their own heat maps. So it's important to choose a couple of them and test them out for accuracy purposes.

The last thing you want is to acquire property and find out that the data that you've relied on was incorrect all along. The more accurate the data, the better. So if there is an area of interest, check it out on various heat maps online.

So how can a heat map help you find income properties? It analyzes your location of interest based on certain filters. These filters include but are not limited to the following:

- Rental income

- Listing price

- Return on investment (ROI)

- Occupancy rate (AirBnB)

Rental income

The heat map filter for rental income will help you determine which areas have the potential to generate the best rental income. Obviously, you want a high rental income (or something reasonable enough to give you a positive cash flow). You may be tempted to find a property that is high on the heat map.

However, it's important to determine your 'cut off number' in terms of how much rental income you want per property. Sometimes, you might just have to settle with a decent number. But rest assured, it may not be the only rental property that you'll invest in.

Numbers add up over time. $1,000 a month becomes $2,000. $2,000 can become $4,000.

You get the idea. So even if you don't land a rental property that's high on the heat map, no need to worry.

Listing price

The listing price filter is based on the price of homes that are currently for sale in the area. The lower the price, the 'warmer' the heat map will indicate. The listing price may be one element of importance to the rental investor.

So it would make sense to go after the properties that have a lower listing price (especially when you are starting out). The heat map will acquire the data based on the prices of houses currently for sale in that area. If you see any properties at a reasonable price, check it out and see if it might be worth using for rental property.

Return on Investment (ROI)

The overall ROI is another great filter worth paying attention to. And for some heat maps, they will do all the number crunching for you so you don't always have to. The heat map will give you a good idea of which properties will give you a good return on investment (and may tell you why).

Occupancy rate for AirBNB

Depending on your area, you may have people looking for a place to crash while they're visiting.

However, they might not have enough money to cough up for a hotel room. Enter AirBNB.

With income properties that are for purchase, you could use it for the purpose of fulfilling the vacancies by way of the AirBNB route. There's a heat map that will determine the occupancy rate of these properties that are ripe for AirBNB. The higher the vacancy rate, that part of the neighborhood will be the perfect spot for people to go to for a place to stay.

And that alone can be a good opportunity to get some extra cash in your pocket. Because people are traveling and want to pay for something that is the fraction of a hotel room. And if your property is in a prime location, what have you got to lose?

Have You Heard Of Multiple Listing Services?

Believe it or not, internet listings are still a thing. And it's all thanks to Multiple Listing Services or MLS. What exactly is an MLS?

It's where properties that are available for purchase or rent are posted throughout various listings on the Internet. Name a real estate search engine like Zillow or even on a real estate website like ReMax and that property will be on there. The listing of the property is bound to be somewhere on the interwebs.

Under an MLS, the listing and selling broker will benefit by putting together the pertinent information and sharing it throughout these listings. MLS listings can be based on a local area or even a much larger region. For example, there could be an MLS strictly for New York City.

If you want to go a step further and go farther out of a metro area, check out a regional listing. So in this case, if you want something outside of New York City proper, you can search through a list that includes properties in New Jersey, Long Island, Southwestern Connecticut, and so on. Not only will you get a much larger list of properties that are available, it gives you the opportunity to open some doors for more options.

Multiple listing services take the guesswork out of which properties are for sale and which ones are not. You can browse through so many real estate websites and you'll see pretty much the same listings if you were to go to another site and search for the same area. As for the MLS itself, the brokers (both representing the buyer and seller) will get a nice commission for every sale that goes through.

One of the best benefits of an MLS is that you get more exposure. Since it's spread out across various listing sites, it will provide you with more traffic (and potentially interested buyers). Compare that to just one broker where the visibility is lesser.

Properties on an MLS must meet certain requirements in order to be on a list. They must be entered within a specific time period. Failure to do so may be grounds for a 'fine' (as will omitting any data that needs to be required for the listing).

The MLS needs to have accurate data, so if you list a rental property that you plan on selling in the future, take note of this. This means getting a specific measurement of the property, how many bedrooms and bathrooms there are, and so on. Also, be sure that the property has high quality photos so interested buyers get a good look at the property from the inside and out.

Opportunities in Direct Mail Marketing

Direct mail marketing may be the oldest and widely practiced thing to do in real estate. Especially when it comes to finding the right kind of rental property. It's worked for many years and still does today (even with modern technology being dominating in almost every industry).

Even though digital marketing reigns supreme, it means that the marketing channel itself will generate a ton of noise. And it will make things a bit more overwhelming. Since almost everyone in real estate is doing digital marketing, the competition is fierce.

And let's not forget, ad blockers are still a thing. So the digital ads may not be within reach of people who want to get rid of those distractions. Those who have been in the business for long know that the roads less traveled often lead to success.

That's where direct mail marketing comes in. Yes, it's a tried and true method that's been around for years. And yet, people look at it and write it off as a bygone thing.

What they fail to realize that the true value of direct mail marketing has never depreciated. A lot of people love getting things in the mail that are not usually considered bills or the like. So you'll want to use this opportunity to stand out.

If you are a rental property owner, you can use this later on when the time comes to sell your property. But what if you are looking to invest in rental property? You can use direct mail as a way to get seller leads better than any digital approach.

Why direct mail?

There are a few reasons why direct mail will work to your advantage. Let's cut to the chase and talk about them:

- **It's less crowded:** As mentioned, a lot of people will rely on digital marketing methods. However, you can take the road less traveled and since a postcard or something similar to someone who may be selling their homes or property. You can leave contact information for them in case they are interested in talking to you more.

- **It can be memorable:** No need to make it snazzy or over the top. When people receive cards or letters in the mail, it can trigger some kind of nostalgia. The feeling of excitement that you got something important in the mail. Direct mail will give it that personalized touch.

- **Wider reach:** Even though the digital approach can provide a laser focused reach, direct mail can reach the people you are interested in contacting as well. However, with direct mail there is a much wider reach. This can pick up the slack where electronic ads tend to miss the mark.

- **Lesser competition:** Where there are less people doing it, the competitive presence is slim. So you can generate success just by doing something that has little to no competitors. It's a hidden gem that people seem to mark off as 'dead' because of modern technology.

A few things to keep in mind while doing mailers. In your mailer, be sure to have a call to action (like a number that they can call or an email to send you a message). You should also define your audience before sending out a piece of mail.

And you should send test batches to ensure that your market is accurately defined. From there, you can measure the amount of engagement as well. The more responsive your audience is, the better.

Also, make sure that your mailers are grammatically correct. Misspellings and grammatical errors will hurt your credibility. Be sure to double check or even triple check before sending things out (even test mailers). And last but not least, don't forget to follow up with the people that you sent your mailers to.

Does direct mail mean neglecting anything that has to do with an online presence? Not at all. In fact, you still want to have a digital presence in order to keep your bases covered.

Considering Wholesale Deals

Wholesale deals are where you can find properties for a lower price. In other words, the wholesale market is 'buy low, sell low'. Wholesaling in real estate is where the property goes under contract and is later assigned to another buyer (who has plans on using the property).

In wholesale deals, there are three people: the buyer, the seller, and wholesaler. The wholesaler acts as the middle man of the deal. When a seller wants to get their property off the market but does not have the essential means to do so, that's when they will connect with a wholesaler.

From there, the wholesaler will find a buyer who will agree to purchase the home at a value that is greater than the seller's asking price. Once the buyer signs the contract, the property is sold. And the wholesaler makes money on the difference.

For example, the seller's asking price would be $250,000. However, the wholesaler finds a buyer who can take it off the seller's hands for about $400,000. The wholesaler in return will get $150,000 for that successful sale (and the seller gets the amount they want).

If you are someone who is looking to buy property at wholesale prices, you may want to see which properties are being sold and for how much. Remember, you will be paying more than what the seller wants. So be sure you have enough cash on hand to purchase the property.

After you purchase the property, you can do what you want with it. You can get some necessary repairs and renovations in. And then you can rent it out to someone who may be looking for a place to live for the long-term.

Smartphone Applications Are Powerful Tools

If you are on the go or in a neighborhood of interest, you can definitely rely on smartphone applications to help find the right property for you. You could be in an area in real time and be close to something that might be your first ever rental property.

What kind of apps are you looking for? It may depend on the kind of property you are going after. For example, if you are looking for an app that will help you find the best residential properties, Zillow or Realtor.com will have mobile apps that you can use. Trulia may also be a good app to have on hand if you are searching for single-family homes.

There are also different apps that will be perfect for when you need to go paperless for signing documents and the like. For this, we recommend an app like DocuSign. You can e-sign contracts, agreements, tenant disclosures, and more. Less paperwork and more convenience right at your fingertips.

Using Online Databases To Find Properties

Online databases are perhaps one of your best alternatives. You can access them both on a mobile or desktop device. Here are a list of online databases that you should consider checking out:

- LoopNet (Note: this is perfect for commercial properties if you are interested in purchasing one as a rental property)

- Auctions.com (great for acquiring foreclosures or even luxury rental properties)

- CraigsList (if you want to look within your local area and beyond)

- Trulia (great for single-family properties and foreclosures)

These are just a sample of online websites and databases that you can check out if you are scouting out potential rental properties. When you spot a property of interest, see if you can get an address so you or your 'scout' can check out the property and see if it's worth looking at further and eventually worth buying.

Final Thoughts

Finding a rental property isn't easy. But it doesn't have to be too complicated. You have a lot of handy apps and websites at your disposal.

Spend time looking through various websites and real estate listings in your local area. Also, take a look at the heatmaps in your area and even miles beyond that. You never know where you'll find your perfect property.

Multiple listings of properties will definitely help you find the right place. And you can even rely on good old-fashioned direct mail marketing to help point you in the right direction. You can send a postcard to home sellers, real estate agents, and other relevant people who can help find your first ever rental property.

Chapter 7 - Dealing With The Numbers

No matter what you invest in, you're going to be dealing with numbers. And that's all part of the process whenever you are planning on getting an excellent return on investment. You don't have to be a math whiz to crunch all the numbers.

And we promise you that we won't throw so many equations that only a genius would figure out. Yes, you'll be dealing with numbers (but we'll do our best to make it as simple as possible). This chapter will be dedicated to how you can run the numbers properly, putting that analysis to good use, and allow yourself to increase your cash flow.

At the same time, we'll show you how you can make an offer and ensure that it will get accepted sooner rather than never. We are approaching what could be one of the most exciting moments of your time as an investor. You are aware of the risks that you're about to take and the rewards that go along with it.

Let's get started and start talking about the numbers:

Do I Really Have To Do An Analysis?

The short answer: yes. The reason why you need to do this is simple. You want to reduce the risk of losing so much in an investment.

Without doing an analysis, you are basically flying blind into the unknown. Nine times out of ten, you'll end up on the losing end rather than the winning one. An analysis of the numbers including the data that will help you figure out whether or not the property you want to rent out is important.

Let us remind you that you'll need to know some numbers including the total return on investment. Aside from that, you want to know about how much the expenses will be and the kind of income that you want to generate to ensure a positive cash flow. Putting those numbers together will help you determine whether or not the property you want to acquire is worth it.

In a previous chapter, we said that there could be one rental property you'll like, but you may come across something better. And by better, we mean a better return on investment. Two separate rental properties in different locations that have the same amenities and the like and one of them could be better than the other.

Remember, the location is usually a huge factor when choosing the right kind of rental property. But keep in mind that you'll need plenty of reliable data to ensure that you are getting the right return on investment rather than some fake numbers. If you need to double check your analysis, you can reach out to members of your team that can confirm whether the numbers are accurate or not.

Running The Number Properly

Now, we get to the good stuff. Running the numbers is not as difficult as you think. It's a necessary task that needs to be done before making the most crucial decisions.

We'll discuss what cash flow is and how you can properly analyze it (along with some other numbers). There are also some things that you'll need to take into consideration as well. When you run the numbers carefully and make sure that everything is accurate and up to date, that will make the deal making process a lot easier.

Now, let's show you how to run the numbers like cash flow and the like:

Calculating your cash flow

As mentioned before, cash flow is what you will be collecting for profit every month after expenses. The goal here is making sure that your cash flow is more than what you spend for expenses every month. That's the key to financial independence.

In case you may have forgotten the formula for calculating your cash flow, here's a quick refresher:

Income - Expenses = Cash flow

See, we told you we weren't going to throw complex equations at you. Your income is your rent that is collected from your tenants. Your expenses include but are not limited to the following:

- Repairs and maintenance

- Mortgage payments

- Property taxes

- Insurance

- Utilities

- Property management

- Vacancies

- Closing costs/filing fees (if applicable)

This is just a sample list of the expenses that you'll want to look at. It's important that you take a look at how much money you plan on spending per month on such things like insurance policies, the mortgage, and the property taxes (since they could change over time). Remember, some of the additional expenses like utilities and services like garbage pickup can be covered by the tenant's rent (which will usually mean the tenant will pay more by default).

Calculating the cap rate

Before you even close the deal, you'll want to consider the cap rate as your best indicator. This will help you determine whether or not the purchase price itself is a good deal on your end or not. With that in mind, let's show you the formula for calculating the cap rate:

Net Annual Income / Purchase Price = Cap Rate

The cap rate will depend on two factors: the area of the property and the state of the market. You'll want to shoot for a cap rate that is 6 percent or above. If the rate is on or above that, you'll have a good deal on your hands.

Now, let's run some numbers in this example:

Let's say you are charging $1,500 a month for rent. The net annual income is the monthly rent multiplied by 12. Therefore: **$1,500 x 12 = $18,000.**

So, you take $18,000 and divide it by the purchase price of the property in question. So let's say this property you want to acquire is $250,000. Is it a good deal if your ideal net annual income?

Let's find out:

$18,000/$250,000 = 7.2

So that rounds to about 7.2 percent. So the cap rate is above the ideal 6 percent. So there you go, that's a deal that you want to put together.

Don't forget the Cash on Cash return

The cash on cash return is the amount of money you'll get for your return on investment. This will depend on how much money you'll put in. Like the cap rate formula, you will be using the net annual income as a way to crunch the numbers.

The formula for calculating the cash on cash return is:

Net Annual Income / Total Cash invested = Cash on Cash Return

Oh...one more thing, the cash on cash return is very similar to the cap rate. So if you purchase the property using cash, you'll get a 7.2 percent return on investment. So remember that the cap rate and the cash on cash return will be the same.

Expenses when buying outright vs. mortgage

So can you purchase the property outright? The short answer is yes. When you purchase the property outright with cash, there is no need to include the mortgage as an expense.

If you want to save a little extra and have a bit more cash flow, then your best bet will be to always purchase the property outright. No mortgage plus interest to deal with. Pretty cool, huh?

But if you are purchasing with the plan to pay a mortgage per month, you should consider consolidating that expense with the interest plus insurance. Sometimes, you may not have all the cash you need to buy property outright (and that's OK).

One thing to keep in mind is that you want to avoid your cash flow going into the negative. The last thing you want is to pay additional expenses out of your pockets. You'll want to put yourself in a situation where the rents are reasonable enough for your tenants (rather than hike them up because you are bleeding cash).

Putting Your Analysis In Action

Now, it's time to put those numbers into action. In this section, we'll show you an extensive example on how to run the numbers so you know that you'll have a positive cash flow for your property. Let's start with the income and expenses using an apartment building as an example:

Income

Number of Units: 10

Average monthly rent per unit: $550

Total monthly income: $5,500

Total annual income: $66,000

Monthly Operating Expenses

Property management: $550 (10 percent of your total monthly income)

Repairs and maintenance: $500

Property Taxes: $350 (per month)

Utilities: $550

Mortgage/Interest/Insurance: $900

Vacancies: $550 (10 percent max of monthly income)

Total monthly operating expenses: $3,400

Net operating income (annual)

Total annual net operating income: $66,000

Total annual net operating expenses: $40,800

Annual net operating income: $25,200

Cap Rate

Note: With the net operating income being $25,200 in this example. Let's say the purchasing price for the apartment building was $400,000.

$25,200 (Annual net income)/ $400,000 (purchase price) = 6.3%

Keep in mind that there is a desired capitalization rate and an actual capitalization rate. This number will depend on how much the actual purchase price of the property is. The offer price will usually differ from the actual purchase price.

Loan expenses

If you have purchased a property using a loan, there are some things to take into consideration when analysing your data. This include the down payment, the loan amount after the down payment itself, acquisition costs and loan fees, and the annual interest rate. Also, the length of the mortgage in terms of years will also be something to take into account.

Cash on Cash Return (ROI)

Remember, the cash on cash return may be the same as the cap rate. However, if you are paying a mortgage or paying off a loan, the number will differ. In one example, let's say that your total annual debt service (or the loan expenses) is $10,000.

So you take the annual operating income and subtract it by the total annual debt service like so:

$25,200 - $10,000 = $15,200

So your annual cash flow will be $15,200. So what about the cash on cash return? It's the net income and your initial investment.

So if you put a $75,000 down payment on the apartment building, you've invested that amount of money up to this point. Therefore:

$25,200 / 75,000 = 33.6

If our calculations are correct, that's a 33.6 percent return on investment from the initial one itself.

Six Ways To Increase Your Cash Flow

Let's say the numbers are not working into your favor. That doesn't mean the end of the world. It should indicate that you'll need to increase your cash flow.

Somehow and some way, you'll get there. With that said, let's take a look at six ways to help you bump up that cash flow so you stay out of the red:

1. Increase the rent

You can increase the rent as you so choose. But as we've stated before, it's better to increase the rent with available vacancies. Yet, if the need is even greater, it may be time to swallow your pride and let your current tenants know what's up.

Depending on where you live, there may be rent control laws that may prevent you from increasing the rent while you have current tenants occupying your units. Before considering the idea of upping the rent, check to see if there are any rent control laws where you are.

2. Consider income from other sources

If increasing rent is out of the question, you could consider the idea of implementing fees for additional services. This may include an on-site laundromat (if you have an apartment building) which will allow people to pay for using the washer and dryer. You could also consider the idea of charging for parking or storage (if your apartment building has these features available).

Depending on the location and what's included on the property, you may need to get creative. If you own a regular apartment building with no parking garage, there is no sense in charging tenants extra for parking.

3. Consider reducing expenses

This can't be said clearly enough. When considering the idea of reducing expenses, you'll need to take into account what you're spending on per month for specific expenses. For example, if you are paying for trash service per month, see if there is another service that offers something for less (which would mean fewer pickups).

Or, let's say you have a property management company that deals with mowing the lawn every month (while charging you for extra monthly services). You can find another property management company that can only charge you for just mowing services and nothing more for less.

4. A larger down payment

At the outset, you may want to put down more money for a down payment when acquiring the property. For example, if your plan to put down $50,000 on a property is hurting the cash flow, consider upping the down payment to perhaps $55,000 or even $60,000.

The more of a down payment you put down, the less likely you'll deal with expenses eating away at your cash flow every month or year.

5. Allow pets

This might be a good time to consider whether or not you want to include pets on the property. If you own an apartment building, including pets may be a good opportunity to generate additional income. That's because you'll be able to charge tenants an extra fee for allowing a pet.

Also, you can decide which pets are allowable and which ones are prohibited. You can even charge a fee based on the size of a dog. A tenant with a chihuahua may pay less than a tenant who owns a husky.

That's all up to you. But think carefully if you want to include pets on your property. Also, keep in mind that there could be potential repair and maintenance. Although we love our pets dearly, they may have accidents or just have a little bit of fun tearing up a place.

6. Make improvements to the building

If you want to increase your cash flow, then why not make some kind of improvements to the property. Something that will increase the overall value of the property such as offering amenities or making widespread renovations. Increasing the overall value may even increase your ROI in return.

Not to mention, you may use these upgrades as an opportunity to provide additional streams of income. As mentioned before, there's a laundromat you can build (if there is enough space), charge for parking, and so on.

Now It's Time To Make An Offer

At this point, you've already run the numbers once or even twice. You've come to the realization that the property you want to purchase will give you a positive income. Now, it's time to make an offer.

So now, you're about to purchase your first ever property. There might be some excitement with a hint of nervousness (which is usually the norm). In this section, we'll discuss how you can make an offer and be able to come out on top.

Will your offer be the right one on the first try? Don't expect it. But once you are able to make an offer that is reasonable, the property will be yours.

Let's take a step-by-step approach on how you can make the best possible offer:

1. Know what you want in a deal

Before entering a deal with someone willing to sell a property to you, you'll want to know what you want. What exactly are you trying to get out of the deal? What are some features of your ideal property that you are looking for?

There are many questions that will come into play such as the location you're aiming for, the type of property that you want to acquire, and so on. You can even whittle it down to when the property was built, how many bedrooms and bathrooms it has, and so on.

It's important to have a criteria for the kind of property you want to acquire. Now that you have spent time putting something together, let's move on to the next step.

2. Compare property already sold in your area to your criteria

If you have an agent, contact then and have them send you information on every property that has been sold in the last six months. From there, you can compare each piece of property against the criteria that you're using for your own acquisition. There are a couple reasons as to why you want to do this.

One, you may look for a similar deal based on some properties that have been sold with the same criteria over that time period. Two, there may be no properties sold at all. In the event of the latter, this might mean making some changes in your criteria such as the area change or the kind of property you want to look for.

3. Make your decision before your next acquisition hits the market

What do we mean by this? You don't need to make an instant decision. You've decided to purchase a property.

Long before the rest of the market knows about it, you can snag the property for yourself without everyone else knowing about it (until after the fact). The sooner you jump on it, the better. You might be lucky enough to get a property that will match your criteria and interest.

4. Make a great offer immediately

The sooner, the better. You can make an offer now as in immediately. You want to pre-prepare and be comfortable with the offer you want to give.

Before doing so, you must be pre-approved by your lender for a loan that is worth the purchase price. Also, you'll want to maintain any liquidity that will allow you breathing room to buy more properties (should you consider expanding your portfolio in the future).

Pick a starting price with the help of your agent. The price may not be the final decision. But your agent will be there to help you acquire the property at a deal that is reasonable and fair for both you and the seller.

Once all is said and done, decide how much money you want to put in escrow. In other words, how much money are you willing to put down as a down payment? These money deposits are usually one to three percent of the purchase price.

Four Tips To Get Your Offer Accepted

To wrap it up, we'll provide you with four tips that will help you get the offer you want. Pay close attention to these if you want the process to be as quick and painless as possible. Check out these tips below:

- **Be 100 percent prepared:** Make sure all of your bases are covered. Get pre-approved for a loan. Analyze the numbers of your target property. And make sure that it's the property you want.

- **Personalize the offer:** If you want to stand out among the crowd, then make the offer more personalized than the generic offers the seller is fielding through. If there is no competition, offer for less than the asking price. If there is competition, come up with an offer that will best the competition. A little negotiating never killed anyone.

- **Protect your acquisition:** After the offer is made, you want to protect yourself from anything that may go sideways. For example, if the seller accepts the offer and later backs out, that can be very painful for you. Instead, consider sending a seller a small deposit. This will give you and the seller a win-win.

- **Never ask the seller to pay the closing costs:** The closing costs should not fall on the seller. As the buyer, you should consider ponying up the extra money to cover it. And it will give the seller a chance to walk away with more cash in their pocket.

Final Thoughts

Now that you know how to analyze the numbers, you can use the formulas listed above to help you find out whether or not you are getting a good deal. Analysis is an absolute must when it comes to investing. You can crunch the numbers and make the determination of whether or not the rent price is just right or if you need to make a few tweaks until you get it right.

Remember, you can also consider a few ideas that will help you increase cash flow as well. If there is no laundromat located at an apartment building that you want to acquire, build one. Not only does that fulfill a need, but it also gives you an additional amount of cash to add onto your income.

Before making an offer, make sure that you know what you want and be prepared to negotiate what should be a fair deal for both you and the seller. Your first offer may go down in flames. So be sure to make your decision before the property you want hits the market.

Not all offers have to be perfect. And they don't have to be ridiculous either.

Chapter 8 - Financing Your Rental Property Investment

Like any other investment, it takes money to get there. However, we're dealing with real estate. So there's a good chance that there will be some financing involved.

You could buy it outright with enough cash. Or maybe you need a loan to put a down payment on it. Either way, you have financing options that are available to you.

In this chapter, we'll talk about financing your rental property and what you'll need to do in order to finance the investment. We'll discuss some of the risks and benefits of doing so. If you are worried about how your loan application will look, this chapter will show you how to get it approved (and we guarantee that it will).

At the same time, we're going to show you how to keep your finances above water. You do not want to make enough mistakes to the point where you'll feel it squeezing your wallet. Too many people have made mistakes while investing in rental property.

But now is your chance to get a deeper understanding of how financing your property works. This is something where many people mess up. But if you follow the steps and tips in this chapter, you'll be ahead of the game.

Let's dive right in:

Do I Need Truckloads Of Cash?

It's easy for us to think that we need a lot of money for a rental property. We often ask: how can we afford this? Indeed, there are expenses that come with the territory of investing in property.

However, we can say that the amount of cash you need will depend on the kind of property you want to acquire. Taking out a loan doesn't always have to be a bad thing. In fact, it might be your best option going forward.

What you need to understand is that it's not a truckload of cash that you need before getting started. It's the ability to get your financial structure in order. Here's what we mean by this:

- **Do you have high-interest debt:** If you have debt that is high in interest, you want to make sure that you get that paid off first. This might be the biggest blemish on your loan application when the time comes to acquire property and something hits a snag. If you have a high-interest credit card that you have yet to pay off, you can do so outright or at least get it to where you have a 0% APR balance transfer.

- **Set up an emergency fund:** An emergency fund will put you a step ahead of a lot of people. We're not joking when we say that there are a lot of people who are unprepared for the unexpected. This emergency fund is basically a general fund that you want to set up just in case the investment itself fails. This 'insurance policy' will protect you against unexpected expenses and financial hardships. How do you set up an emergency fund? Consider setting aside enough money that will cover no less than six months worth of expenses. Keep it in a bank account that you can easily access.

Having enough money to buy a rental property again will depend on the property. Clearly, it takes more money to purchase a $400,000 apartment building than a $150,000 single-family house. But what about the down payment?

The down payment is something you need. But it's not the only thing that you will need money for. You'll also need money to pay for any closing costs (since you don't want to place that burden on the seller).

But let's not stop there. You also need enough money set off to the side for repairs and maintenance. And lastly, there's also money you need for reserves.

The reserves are basically enough to hold you over due to vacancies and the like. To get an idea of how much money you need to put in a reserve account, consider putting in six to 12 months worth of mortgage payments inside a reserve account.

Simply put, you can afford a rental property if you have the financial discipline to do so. We can't define what consists of a 'truckload of cash'. But we will say that you need enough for a down payment and enough to help cover any of the necessary expenses like mortgage payments and repairs.

Ways To Finance Your Investment

There are so many ways to finance your rental property. Yet, it circles back to one word: loans. What kind of loans are out there for rental properties and the like?

Which loan will you need for your property? These questions we'll answer shortly. But after you read this section, you'll get a good understanding of the types of loans that are available.

You may take out one for your first property and take out a different type of loan for any of your subsequent acquisitions. It all depends on what you want to include in your real estate portfolio. Let's take a look at the types of loans that are available to you and why they are important:

Conventional mortgage loans

The first loan will be taking a look at the conventional mortgage loans. These are the most common investment property financing options that are usually issued to real estate investors. Especially if they are focusing on residential properties like apartments or single-family homes.

If you own your own home, chances are you took one out when you purchased it. A conventional mortgage loan is usually offered by a bank or a mortgage broker. Obtaining a mortgage will depend on the state you reside in (assuming you live in the United States).

If you are a property investor, you'll want to put down as much as 20 percent of the property's purchase price as a down payment. For example, let's say the property you want to purchase has a price tag of $300,000. The down payment itself will be $60,000 at minimum.

Don't forget that your credit score and your history will either make or break your chances for getting approved for a conventional mortgage loan. That's why we mentioned paying off any high interest debt you may have before considering a purchase of a property.

If you have a credit score of 620 or higher, then you will likely obtain a conventional mortgage loan. However, if you are aiming for a good interest rate, a credit score of 740 will probably help you. Also, having six months of cash reserves will also give you a leg up in making sure you qualify for a loan.

Hard money loans

Hard money loans are given to investors by individuals or companies that lend you money specifically for the purpose of investing in properties. The good news about these loans is that they are much faster to acquire. Not only that, these lenders don't look at your credit score.

So if you find that acquiring a conventional mortgage loan may not be in the cards, consider getting a hard money loan. However, there is one caveat to keep in mind. These loans are short-term loans.

Specifically, the life of these loans will be up to 36 months. On top of that, these loans command high-interest rates. For this reason, this kind of loan may not be suitable for any rental property. These may be used if you plan on snagging properties that have a low price tag (or if you want to buy the property and flip it after making improvements).

If you are planning on acquiring a long-term investment property, then a hard money loan may not be the route to take.

Private Money Loans

Unlike hard money loans, private money loans are not provided by those who are hard money lenders. This is one other alternative route should you be rejected for a conventional mortgage loan by a bank. This loan is for individuals who have a good amount of money set off to the side and aim for a good return on their investment property.

These private money lenders may even be in your existing network. This network can include friends, family members, or even real estate investors you have managed to connect with along the way.

These loans are secured by way of a promissory note or an existing mortgage on the property.

Keep in mind that the private money lender can have the power to foreclose the property if the loan payment isn't paid off by a specific deadline. So be sure to honor your promise to pay back the loan in the best arrangement possible.

Fix-and-Flip Loans

Fix and flip loans are aimed towards property investors that want to purchase a property, fix it up to increase the overall value, and then sell it for a profit (or flip it). These are short-term loans, so the interest rates will likely be higher compared to other loans.

That's why flippers will need a short amount of time to renovate the house and sell it. And they can do so in the quickest way possible. They'll have the money to pay off the loan and keep the rest if they wish.

Like hard money loans, it's easy for them to get approved. Lenders can look at your credit score, but will not use it as part of their decision making process. They want to make sure that the property you are acquiring has potential profitability.

These loans will usually take a year or less to pay off. So if you are a flipper, you don't need to worry about lenders tracking you down unless you have a reason to worry.

Home equity loan

Home equity loans are another common loan that will be used by investment property owners. If you plan on purchasing a single-family rental property, this might be one worth considering (since it may be considered a loan for getting a second home). The loan will be based on the difference between the homeowner's equity and the current market value of the property itself.

The lender will run a credit check and will appraise your home to ensure that you have the right creditworthiness to secure a loan. This kind of loan is easy to obtain and will provide you with a good source of cash when you need it. The interest paid on these loans are tax-deductible, so that will come in handy when it comes time to file.

If you are a property investor that plans on being responsible when it comes to handling the finances, this kind of loan will work to your advantage. You'll know how much you'll need to borrow (while the investment itself will be a reliable source of income so you can repay it).

Commercial investment loans

Suppose you want to go down the road of commercial investing. No problem. Just apply for a loan that focuses on commercial real estate.

Like the residential loans, you'll have loans such as hard money loans (from lenders that specialize in commercial real estate) and conventional loans as well. The only differences are the down payments, the length of the loan, and the interest rates. Let's take a look at the numbers for these kinds of loans.

For one, the down payment will range anywhere between 15 to 35 percent of the purchase price. Second, the financing options will range anywhere from 12 to 36 months. And lastly, the interest rates will run between 8 to 13 percent.

Depending on your current financial situation and the type of property that you want to acquire, there's a good chance that one of these loans will be a big help to you. As you start your career as a real estate investor, you'll understand how each of these loans work and what you need in order to qualify for them.

Be sure to take a look at your credit score and set aside money for your cash reserves. Before you even apply, look over any of the requirements. They may vary from one lender to the next, but you need to double check to see if you have things in order before being approved.

What are the Risks and Benefits?

Like all kinds of investing, there are risks and benefits. And you need to be aware of them when you are beginning your journey as a real estate investor. Knowing the risks and benefits will keep you a step ahead of the others.

This will usually pertain to loans and the like. While there are benefits, people tend to forget about the risks that are a part of them. Let's take a look at the risks first:

- **Short-term loans equal higher interest:** You may have noticed a pattern over the course of the previous section. A short-term loan will usually yield a higher interest. Therefore, you should consider your options carefully about the types of loans you quality for. Higher interest rates could mean a higher amount of money that you'll need to pay if you miss a loan payment (or continuously fail to pay it on time).

- **You may get rejected repeatedly due to credit score:** It happens. And all you lose is time. So be sure to check out what requirements you meet (and which ones you fall short of) prior to applying for a loan.

Now, let's take a look at the benefits:

- **Loans are temporary:** Yes, these bank loans are temporary. Which means they won't last as long as you live. Once you pay off the loan, you own the investment property outright (which means less expenses).

- **Interest is tax deductible:** As mentioned earlier, the interest that you pay on the loan is tax deductible. Which is perfect for when you want to reduce the tax bill that you get every year from Uncle Sam. The less taxes you pay because of these deducibles, the better.

- **You maintain control of your investment:** The bank doesn't control the investment. Nor do they take any ownership position in your business. This means you make the decisions on what you can do with the property. The bank cannot say 'hey, let's build a laundry facility on the property'. Nor can they have a say in which tenants can move in and who can't rent a place.

The Guaranteed Way To Get A Loan Approved

If you want to get your loan approved, then pay close attention to this section. While loans may be hard to attain for the average real estate investor, it might not be hard for you. You need to put yourself at an advantage to where lenders see you as someone who is responsible and ahead of the curve.

In order to be guaranteed approval for a loan, you'll need to consider the following:

- **Make sure your credit is good:** Your credit score will be the difference between getting approved for a loan or getting rejected. Your credit score will be impacted by the following factors: payment history, outstanding balances, length of credit history, the types of accounts you have, and the credit inquiries. Sometimes, a credit score may not outright deny you. But the size of the loan may be smaller than what you want. Also, consider a credit audit as well as dispute any inaccurate information, late charges, and the like that may have caused your credit to take a nosedive.

- **Pay off any debt:** This can't be stressed enough. Any debt that you may have will carry on you like a weight. Obtaining a property loan will be based on the debt-to-income ratio. Lenders will take a look at how much you make and compare it to how much you can spend. If the debt is 35 percent or more of your total income, you will be rejected. Reduce the debt as far off as possible before you even consider applying.

- **Make a determination of what you can afford:** Consider an accurate number of what you can afford in terms of the properties you want to acquire. Depending on the lender, there will be guidelines in place of how much money you can borrow (minimum or maximum). Also, you'll want to consider your current and future finances as you are starting out.

- **Compile your work history:** Your work history will be looked at by your lenders. Ideally, they'll give a plus to anyone who has worked two or more years in a single job. The work history will verify that you have a reliable source of income. This may also determine the level of risk you may be eligible for.

- **Gather other income information:** Aside from work history, you may want to consider gathering any information where income is generated. This includes any bank statements, tax returns, pay stubs, statements from brokers, and more.

- **Down payment:** The down payment is the amount of money you'll want to put down. As mentioned before, it can take up to 20 percent of the purchase price. At the lowest, it can be 3 percent.

- **Compare lenders:** As mentioned before, the guidelines and requirements can vary from one lender to the next. Pay close attention to what they are so you can determine which lender will approve you and which ones may reject you due to not meeting one or multiple requirements.

- **Get pre-approved:** When you are pre-approved for a loan, this places you at an even greater advantage. Not only will you be viewed favorably by the seller, it will also make the process a lot easier.

Tips To Keep Your Finances Afloat

If you want to keep your finances above water, these tips will help you out. It's important to know about these so you are able to keep your head in the game and not run into any issues. These are the following tips:

- **Put down at least 20 percent:** Yes, we mentioned the down payment can be as low as 3 percent. But you're better off putting down 20 percent of the purchasing price anyways. Because the sooner you pay it off, the better.

- **Don't expect getting the same rate:** Mortgage rates may differ when compared between primary home mortgages and what you could borrow for rental properties.

- **Keep your credit score clean:** 640 is good. But if you keep it in between 670 to 739, then you have an even better shot at landing a loan.

- **Know that not every lender is alike:** Again, the requirements are different. One lender can give you $100,000 while another can give you $75,000 at max. Remember to determine how much you can actually afford.

- **Your finances do get a little tricky:** The banks will consider your debt-to-income ratio and the cash reserves you may have. So it's important to keep your debts low and make sure you have enough cash in your reserves to cover expenses should things don't go as planned.

Final Thoughts

Being able to finance your rental property investment is easier than you think. However, if you have unpaid debts and the like, it might be difficult to get approved. But do not despair, because you have more than one option.

The type of loan you want to get will depend on the type of property you are willing to acquire. You may qualify for one loan, but not for another. Choose the loan that will work best for you based on your current financial situation.

Once you've acquired the property and have managed to generate a good amount of income, you can then refinance it and pay off the loan if you so choose (and we'll show you a cool way to do that in the next chapter). In the meantime, pay off whatever debts that you may have and clear up any credit issues.

When you finally get that squared away, that should give you a good chance at getting approved for a loan.

Chapter 9 - The BRRRR Strategy: No It is Not A Cold

BRRRR. Is it cold in here? No, it's not.

But the one cold thing that we'll be talking about is the cold hard cash you might be getting every month from your rental properties. Before you do, we're going to talk about a strategy known as the 'BRRRR' strategy. This is a method that is making its rounds amongst the real estate world.

In this chapter, we'll explain what it is and how to use it step-by-step. We'll also discuss the main risks that are involved with this strategy. And lastly, we'll discuss how to use it as one of the investing methods that you can use every time you have your eye on a rental property.

At this point, you're unsure of what kind of strategy you want to use in order to snag the property you want. However, this is one in particular that you might like since it's simple, detailed, and easy to follow. The last thing you want to do is find a strategy that is complicated and will cause you to lose one deal after another.

We encourage you to follow along in this chapter so you have a good idea of what to do and how to get the deals you want using this strategy every single time you do it. Let's get right to it:

The Famous BRRRR Method

The BRRRR Method stands for the following: buy, rehab, rent, refinance, repeat. Read that over again as many times as you need too. This is the strategy and framework that rental investors typically use when they want to generate passive income using properties.

It sounds simple enough, right? And the strategy is basically the words in the order that they appear. You can't mix them up nor switch one 'r' with another.

This method just might be your go-to strategy whenever you want to invest in properties more than once. And it's a sure fire way to help increase your cash flow while solidifying your portfolio over time. If you are looking for a roadmap towards financial independence with no shortcuts, this is exactly what you want on hand (and you can repeat the process as many times as you need to).

Examining BRRRR: Buy, Rehab, Rent, Refinance, & Repeat

In this section, we are going to break down every bit of BRRRR so you understand what to do in the process. This is something that you can do repeatedly over and over again until you feel like you've acquired enough property for your portfolio. As mentioned before, this is a straightforward roadmap that takes you from point A to point E (ABCDE not ACDEB or any ridiculous combo).

It's important to follow this strategy from the beginning so you have all your bases covered before moving on to the next stage. Once you get the hang of it, you'll be able to repeat the process over and over again. Let's break it all down:

Buy

This part is obviously self-explanatory. You buy the property outright with cash or with a financing method like a loan (which we've outlined in the previous chapter). Ideally, the buy strategy here requires a specific kind of property.

It's a property that is in need of some repairs or renovations. In plain English, you're looking for a fixer-upper. So you'll want to purchase a property that you can be able to acquire at a below market price.

As mentioned, you can purchase it with enough cash on hand. However, should you go the financing route, there are some loans that are perfect for this kind of property. Specifically, go for the hard money, private money, or even the fix and flip loans.

The reason why you want to consider these loans is because you'll be able to acquire the money fairly quickly without a credit check. On top of that, the loans are short-term. But that will give you plenty of time to repair the property and pay off the loan in time.

We'll show you exactly how to go about doing that plus more when we talk about the 'refinancing' part of this strategy.

Repair

After you've acquired the property, that's when you can be able to repair it, rehabilitate it, or renovate it (depending on the needs). That's when you'll need to be investing in quite a bit of money. Before the repairs begin, you want to thoroughly examine the house from top to bottom.

What are some things that are urgently in need of repair? Are there some hidden issues that exist (such as structural damage)? You'll want to inspect the property yourself or have a professional do it before repairs or renovations are made.

Ideally, you should at least take a look at the property before you even buy it. That way, you'll know ahead of time how much money you can put in for repairs and renovations. Once you have a good ballpark estimate, you can go from there.

Remember, repairs and renovations will increase the property value. So if you put in a good amount of work into it, you'll be able to make it attractive enough for the appraiser to put a high value price tag on it.

It will certainly work to your advantage when the time comes to rent it out or even sell it outright. Don't forget, with increased value you can also better your chances of refinancing the property. Before you do that, let's talk about how you can get there.

Rent

The repairs and renovations have been made and the place looks like it's in good shape. So now, you need to fulfill the vacancy with a reliable and trustworthy tenant. The process can take a bit of time (or it can take awhile).

This can also depend on the property you have acquired. If the property is a single-family home, then it shouldn't be a lot of trouble to find a tenant. However, if it's an apartment building that has been renovated, that could take some time (and a bit of screening to find the right tenants).

In the event if you are fulfilling multiple vacancies, you'll need a property manager to help field through the pool of applicants to help you decide which tenants are reliable and which ones may be rejected due to the policy requirements that they don't meet.

Without tenants that pay, you get no income from the rental property. That can't be simple enough to say.

Refinance

Now this is one of the fun parts about the BRRRR strategy. This is where all the hard work pays off. Because you now have a source of steady, consistent income in a rental property. This will allow you to let the lenders know that you have equity in the property and you can do a cash-out refinance.

The cash-out refinance will be used to pay off the hard money loan (or other loan) that you used to acquire the property in the first place. At that point, you can be able to reduce the expenses and have an increased cash flow.

So, what are you going to do at this point? Is one property enough? Do you want to snag another rental property and increase your portfolio?

There's only one simple answer to those questions.

Repeat

Yup. You repeat the process. And the best way to go about doing that is using whatever leftover profit from the cash-out refinance to do the whole thing over and over again.

This includes putting a new down payment on your next rental property. And as a result, you get increased cash flow and enough money to balance out all of your expenses. This seems pretty easy to do, right?

However, there are some caveats and snags that you may run into with this strategy (which will discuss in a little bit).

The 4 Main Things To Consider

Before you even go through with the strategy, it is important to consider the four main things about this strategy. This will make the approach a lot easier rather than miss a step (and not even realize it). The

BRRRR strategy can work to your advantage if done properly.

With that in mind, let's take a look at the four main things you'll want to consider before you even buy the property:

1. How much money will you actually need

This can't be said better than it already is. You'll want to know how much money you will need for the initial purchase of the property. Not to mention, you'll need to consider how much you'll need for the repair (or renovation/rehabilitation) of the property.

You may already have some money set off to the side for the purpose of repairing or rehabilitating it. And all you need now is a loan for a down payment. So get a good idea of how much money in total you need for your first property and how much of a budget you'll need to repair or rehab the property.

Also, one more reason why you should inspect the property before even buying it is to determine how much money you need for the repairs themselves. Get a good estimation from your perspective (and perhaps get a second opinion from a home inspector who might just catch what you've missed).

2. How long will it take to repair or renovate

The time it takes to repair or renovate will also be another thing to consider. Not only will you be aware of what needs to be fixed, but you'll also need to be prepared for any unexpected surprises. Once you assess the initial repairs and renovation plans, you'll get a good idea of how long the entire project will take.

The scope of the project will depend on the size of the property. It will possibly take less time for a single-family property to be repaired or renovated compared to a small apartment building. So keep this in mind whenever you are searching for a property.

3. What will be the right rental amount

Obviously, you'll come to a point where you'll need to set the rate of rent. How much will the tenant pay per month to ensure it will be enough to cover expenses on your end (while maintaining a positive cash flow)? Remember to use the formulas in the previous chapter to determine that the rent rate you desire will meet your cash flow needs.

There may be rental rates that are too low and others that are too high. So you really want to find the sweet spot. One caveat would be to find a tenant who would be willing to pay that amount of rent every month.

It takes the right tenant to fulfill the vacancy. They pay on time, have a solid source or income, and will cause you no headaches at all at three in the morning (unless there is an urgent repair or if something is actually happening like a fire).

4. What will be the appraisal after the fact

After you've put in the money for repairs, found a tenant, and get a good stream of income as a result, now the appraisal process begins. This will play a role in how you will be able to refinance the property (and eventually pay off the loan).

What if the appraisal comes up short? What may be the cause of it? There are some things that could play a role in getting an appraisal that might be not what you expect.

Look no further than the current market itself. In a strong market, you'll probably get an appraisal that is exactly what you want in terms of value (or more).

The market could take a downturn while you are in the process of renovating the property.

When you're in the early stages of the BRRRR method, it's important to watch the market and see how it holds up. Because a change in the market can make or break your chances of getting a better return on investment. As you move from one stage to the next, take a look at how the market is doing.

You may not get the appraisal that you want. But be outcome dependent and have options in case you get an appraisal that you want (or didn't expect).

Using BRRRR as an Investing Method

Before using the BRRRR as a method for building your portfolio, we'll be discussing the advantages and disadvantages. This is the one approach that we highly recommend for newbies starting out. You'll want to acquire your first rental property (and subsequent properties after that) using this method if you so choose.

Let's start with the following advantages:

Advantages

- **Your ROI is scalable:** You can easily scale up your return on investment. The best way to do that is to acquire additional properties. You can even acquire properties with as little investment as possible. Heck, depending on how much extra cash you have lying around you could acquire your next properties with cash.

- **A proven formula:** Indeed, the BRRRR method is a tried and true formula that can be repeated over and over again. There is no tweaking or major changes needed. It's even proven to work over and over again regardless of the economic and market conditions.

- **Excellent rewards and benefits:** A lot of money in your pocket, more chances and opportunities to get more properties, and the ability to get people to manage the properties for you while you step away from the day to day operations. The BRRRR method could be exactly what you need to follow in order to achieve financial freedom and freedom from the heavy lifting that occurs with day-to-day operations.

Disadvantages

- **Repair/renovations may go over budget:** You might already have a set budget for

186

renovations and repairs. However, you may come across some new things to fix. And that could mean more added time and money. That's why you want to do a thorough inspection (or get a second opinion from a home inspector) before deciding how much you'll want to spend on repairs and renovation.

- **Repairs/renovations could take longer:** Tying to the previous point, new needs for repair can take a bit of time. And it could extend the schedule. So the time you estimate for these repairs and renovations can be a little off.

- **Vacancies may take longer to fulfill:** This may depend on the property. And it also may depend on the rent you've set it to. Either way, you won't be able to fulfill it immediately. It takes time to find the right tenant. So be patient and you will eventually find one.

Final Thoughts

The BRRRR Strategy will be your roadmap to building your rental property empire. As easy as it is to follow along, there are some disadvantages that you'll run into. Not only that, you'll need to follow the strategy to a tee and not make any shortcuts in the process.

You now have a proven formula that will help you easily acquire a property and be able to find the right kind of financing options. At first, you'll likely need a loan like a hard money loan. After putting in the money for repairs and renovations, you can get a tenant and earn income for the property.

At that point, you can refinance, pay off the loan, and repeat the process all over again. It's the simplest way to build your portfolio and increase your cash flow in the process. But you'll want to follow the steps carefully as you go.

So through the motions when you are in the buying process. Be thorough and know exactly what needs repairing. And finally, get a tenant that will be able to pay the rent on time every month.

There is no strategy quite like this. And it's even the perfect formula for beginners.

Chapter 10 - Going With A Long Distance Investment

Sure, it might be nice to find a property in your local area. But there will come a time when the pickings will be quite slim. It might be to the point where you'll need to go outside of your localized area (even way out of it).

Is it a good idea to go with a real estate investment that might be a longer distance from you? That's for you to decide. But we'll talk about that in more detail in this chapter (and why a long distance investment might benefit you).

There are experienced real estate investors that not only have local rental properties, but they do have some out of the state as well. But you will still have the money coming from tenants that you can easily access. And you will also have someone who is overseeing the property when you are not in the area.

So a long distance investment may not be a bad thing at all. And you don't even have to be in the area often. If you are looking for a great way to find rental properties, it's better to find something that is actually out of the way.

Let's go long distance and talk about why finding an investment outside of your local area might just be what you need to do to get started:

Not Everything Is In Your Backyard

As mentioned earlier, you may have tough luck finding the property you want in your local area. And it can get to the point where the selections are so slim that you'll need to go farther. It's OK to have a property that may be hundreds of miles away or a few states over.

One of the reasons why a long distance investment is so important is that you can get more bang for your buck elsewhere. Sure, you can get a rental property in larger cities (where the rents are high). But the expenses of acquiring the property may be even higher.

Instead of purchasing a rental property inside the city limits, your next step up is the suburbs. However, if there is nothing doing out that way, going much farther would be sufficient. Think about it, a 100 unit apartment building in New York City may cost you more than one that is located somewhere in Pennsylvania.

Yes, you can find the same kind of apartment building and pay less just by switching up the location. At some point, you may have just enough money to purchase properties in the city. Then again, even if you do have the money those properties could be hard to come by.

Long distance rental property investing is great because you can purchase a property from an area that's far away from you. And you don't have to be there all the time to manage it. On top of that, the farther you go, the more opportunities you'll have.

This will allow you to open the door to possibly starting your rental property empire sooner rather than later. You'll be able to build out a portfolio and at least get the attention of local sellers at some point. Rather than wait for a local property, you can build a reputation of being a good landlord sooner with a long-distance property investment.

You'll have a few good references as well such as the property manager you hire to take care of the property itself. You'll also have others that will go to bat for you. These are people who you build a professional relationship with and they trust you with everything in terms of property management.

There's also passive income too

No matter where the property is, you can still earn passive income. It's not like you cannot access your fund outside of where the property is. But it's going to take some careful planning to adopt a financial model that is reasonable and realistic.

You still need to determine the rent price, the expenses, and everything in between to ensure that you get positive cash flow. At the same time, you'll want to find someone who is responsible and is able to handle everything from tenant requests to setting up a relationship with contractors, landscaping businesses, and more. You and your property manager can talk on the phone or even use video chat to make decisions regarding the property itself.

Yes, having a long-distance property does have it's own challenges. But believe us when we say that it's not as bad as some people think. As long as you have the right kind of people dealing with your property on a regular basis, you don't have to worry.

It Isn't As Risky As You Think

One of the biggest concerns about investing long-distance is that you might be taking a huge risk. Some will even go so far to say that you might be getting scammed. Sure, there may be some truth, but there is a difference between playing it smart and just handing over money to someone without thinking twice (or seeing the property first hand).

There are a few reasons why long-distance investments are no longer as risky as they used to be. You'll be able to make determinations of whether or not the property is worth the investment just by looking at the data. Not to mention, you have reliable sites like Trulia and Zillow to help you find the property of your dreams.

Obviously, the number one key when it comes to all investments is doing your due diligence. This task will help you determine whether or not the property is the real deal or if it's a property that might be a scam. Doing your due diligence will reduce all kinds of risks that could lead you to getting screwed over.

Also, you can get video confirmation of the property and get a good idea of what it looks like from the inside. It's a lot better than having to travel a lengthy distance to see it for yourself. You can even talk about the property with the seller over the phone or via Skype (or Zoom).

Another thing that you'll want to pay attention to is the online reviews. Look through them thoroughly. Although some of the positive reviews are short, it's hard to take them at face value. If the positive reviews are detailed and slightly longer, take those a little bit seriously.

The negative reviews is something you'll want to pay attention to as well. Again, the detailed reviews will give you an explanation as to why someone would leave negative reviews. That will give you a good idea to find a different property.

As long as you do your research and your due diligence, you'll find the property you want. From there, you can go through the motions using the BRRRR method as outlined in the previous chapter. But what if there needs to be repairs?

That's when you'll need a property manager to handle all of that. Have someone local onsite oversee the repairs while the contractors work on it. They can handle the expenses after you send them money (or you can yourself once they bill you).

Important Steps To Take When Investing in Other Places

If you plan on investing in a long-distance property, it's always a good idea to consider taking as many important steps as possible. Not only will you do your best to cover your bases, but you'll make sure that everything is done properly. Even if you won't be physically on the property, you still want to play it smart as far as investing and managing your properties are concerned.

We'll be taking a look at seven tips that you'll want to follow. These will help you in the long run if you are starting out with your rental property career by choosing a property outside of where you live. These are some of the things to take into consideration:

1. Find a property manager you can trust

A property manager will handle everything from which tenants can move in to overseeing maintenance and repairs while you are not in the area. This is someone who will perform the day-to-day operations. They will keep you in the loop on what's been going on regularly.

Both you and the property manager will discuss the policies on what kind of tenants are allowed and what could deny them from moving in. The property manager will also relay any information regarding repairs, unexpected expenses, and so on.

2. Build your network with people located in that area

You might already have a local network of real estate investors, property managers, and so on.

However, since you have property in a long-distance area, you'll need to repeat the same process. This time, you can network with those in the local area who handle repairs and maintenance and other important tasks that pertain to the property.

When you are in the area where the property is located, you'll know people in the area rather than nobody at all. If something happens on your property, you'll know who to call. It's nice to have connections in every place where you have a rental property.

3. Consider automation where appropriate

We live in a time where automation is possible for mundane, repetitive tasks. One such thing that can be automated is the rent payments from the tenant. You can make arrangements where a tenant will pay their rent every month using methods like wire transfer.

This way, you won't need to worry about tracking people down and receiving physical checks from them on a regular basis. Post-dated checkers are still an option as well. You can receive those checks from tenants and be able to cash them every first of the month.

If there is a task that is menial and is usually repetitive, chances are it can be automated.

4. Communicate often

This can't be stressed well enough. Communicate with your property managers, the tenants, and the people that are working to keep your property in ship shape. A phone or video call goes a long way.

Also, if you plan on traveling to the area, let your tenants and other personnel know ahead of time. The same way when it's the other way around. That way, you will all know where everyone is so you can be able to get in contact with them face to face should the opportunity to do so arrives.

5. Do a regular inspection

You can do a regular inspection without having to travel. That's when your property manager can be your extra set of eyes in terms of finding possible issues with the property (and assigning a contractor to make said repairs). You as a landlord should reserve the right to do inspections on a regular basis.

Even when you have an on-site property owner to do it for you, you'll know about the condition of the property every single time. When repairs are needed, either you or the property manager will make the call to get the right people over to take care of the issue.

6. Always get insurance coverage

Insurance is a must-have for any property whether it's local or long-distance. You may be able to cover every property you'll invest in under the same policy (depending on who insures you). That's because disaster can strike anywhere.

Yes, it can also happen on properties that are far away from where you live. Find an insurance company that can be able to assist you in terms of covering your properties no matter where they are located. Having it all under one policy rather than have multiple policies at the same time can be easy when handling all of your expenses.

7. Set the terms and the policies

The terms and policies must always be set. This is to ensure that the tenants follow them. You will have a property manager that must be willing to enforce them.

It's your property, and it's your rules. You want these to be as clear as possible before any tenant moves in. This includes whether or not smoking is allowed on the property or if you can allow pets in the units (assuming it's an apartment building).

Final Thoughts

A long distance property might be one of your best options when you're starting out. You may have the worst luck finding property in your local area. You will come to the realization that sometimes, starting out local won't be a reality.

Not to worry, you will invest in local properties at some point. But if you want to start building your rental property empire sooner rather than later, you'll want to get out of your local area and see how far you can go. The perfect property is out there, even if it's hundreds of miles away (or in the next state over).

Investing in real estate properties from a long-distance away isn't as risky as it once was. Thanks to technology, you'll be able to know what you're getting into. And you'll be able to do the due diligence to ensure whether or not it's a worthy investment.

Follow the seven tips that we've outlined above and you'll find that investing and managing a rental property from afar isn't all that bad. You'll still get a good amount of money to help your cash flow. As long as you have the right kind of people handling your property, you'll be in good shape.

Chapter 11 - A Choice In Management

One of the biggest tasks for having a rental property is managing it. While you have the option to manage it yourself, you also have another choice to have someone else do it. Let's face it, you're not going to be on all of your properties at the same time.

So now, it comes down to whether or not you should manage it yourself or rely on a property manager that you can trust to do it for you. In this chapter, we'll discuss when is a good time to choose either option. At this point, you might have already made your choice.

We'll be taking a look at whether or not if you can self-manage your properties (while weighing the pros and cons). We'll also discuss the same in terms of when you want to get someone else to do the job for you. Either way, one choice will be easier than the other.

When you invest in multiple properties, the choice is pretty much a no brainer 90 percent of the time. This chapter will alleviate any concerns you may have in regards to property management. Let's get right to it:

Choosing Between Self-Management and Property Management

As a property investor, you'll be faced with the choice of managing the property yourself or having someone else do it. When you already have multiple properties under your belt, the choice will lean towards more property managers compared to managing them yourself.

It doesn't matter if you are the greatest multi-tasker in the world. You can't always be on all of your properties at the same time. And you may find running around from one property to the next to be quite stressful.

This might work to your advantage if you don't mind running around from one end of town to the other. That is if your properties are all located in the same town. However, you could have properties spread out by five miles from each other.

As mentioned before, you may also have long distance properties. Obviously, you cannot make the trip that will be hundreds of miles away. If it's a long distance property, you have no choice but to have a property manager oversee the day-to-day operations (unless you intend to move to that location in the future).

We'll be taking a look at the pros and cons of self-management as well as having someone else do it for you. After this, you'll be able to make a decision with ease. You could manage one property by yourself and have the rest of them managed by other people.

Or you can have the properties all managed by one company and you can just sit back and collect the passive income once a month. It's all up to you. Let's move on and discuss the idea of self-managing your properties.

Can You Self-Manage Your Properties?

Self-managing is defined as maintaining the properties yourself. This means you are responsible for approving or rejecting tenant applications. You will also perform the day to day operations as a property manager.

This may be one of your best options if you are planning on focusing on one property from the start. If the property is in your local area, it will be a lot easier to manage it yourself. Especially when you have plenty of time throughout the day.

Take a look at the pros and cons below so you'll make a decision on whether or not self-managing is right for you. Let's start with the pros:

Pros of self-management

- **You have more control:** Of course, you have even greater control over your property if you manage it yourself. Just because you decide that you let someone else manage it, doesn't mean you lose your 'final say' on what happens to the property. This is more apt towards the day to day operations.

- **Closer relationships with tenants:** When you manage the property yourself, you'll be mostly in contact with the tenants. You'll see them on a daily basis. However, you may be dealing with tenant issues that could hurt the relationship. Do your best to make it healthy and productive on your end.

- **You'll save money:** You'll save yourself money on an expense that would otherwise go towards your property manager. Ten percent of what you earn per month will usually go towards property management.

- **You gain knowledge and experience:** You will learn about your property both inside and out. Plus, you'll get experience and know-how in terms of managing a property. That way, you can train the right person whenever you want to rely on someone else to manage your additional properties.

Cons of self-management

- **It can be stressful:** Yes, handling the day-to-day tasks of managing a property can be stressful. Especially if you are handling multiple properties at once. Imagine getting a call at 2AM from a tenant regarding a broken pipe. Then, you'll need to figure out how to take care of it as soon as possible. Other stressors include unreliable tenants and the like.

- **It requires time:** Yes, it will require time out of your day to manage the property. Even one managing one property will require a good amount of time out of your day. If you manage multiple properties, the responsibilities will multiple.

- **Rent may be too low or too high:** You may set the rent price and it may be too low for the average market or too high for your ideal tenant to pay. If you know a good reasonable price when you see it, that's when you can set it and go from there.

Taking The Steps Toward A Successful Management

Successful management isn't easy. But it can be done. It's important to follow these tips below so you can be able to manage your properties with ease (whether it's by yourself or via a manager).

If you are doing self-management, follow these tips and be able to train your property manager so the both of you can be on the same page in terms of how the business is run. Let's take a look at the following:

1. Automate the process

Automation is possible whenever you or someone else is managing the property. There are different tools that you can use to automate tenant payments, issue order tickets for repairs, and tedious administrative tasks that a property manager does quickly and repeatedly.

Find the tasks that are automated and find the appropriate apps and software that will allow the automation process to work like it's supposed to.

2. Pick the right rental rate

You'll be dealing with the numbers on a regular basis. This is because you want to keep your cash flow above water. So finding the right rental rate that is fair for both you and your tenant is essential.

Consider the market averages in your area and start from there. The right rental rate could draw in tenants quicker compared to units or properties that command a higher rent.

3. Screen your tenants with diligence

You want to screen your tenants for a few things. This includes reliability of payment, whether they are known for respecting the property, and other requirements that you'll want for an ideal tenant. The last thing you want to be is lax in who you want in a tenant since there are some bad apples out there.

You want your properties to be a safe place. So you might not be apt to allow career criminals to become tenants on your property. Think about the kind of tenants you want on your property and the ones you want to steer clear from.

4. Brush up on landlord-tenant laws

Just so you are on the same page with your tenant, you'll want to learn about landlord-tenant laws. This way, you want to make the right moves rather than make a wrong one that can get you into legal trouble. One other way to go about doing this is adding an attorney to your network.

This should be an attorney who is familiar with landlord-tenant laws. This is someone who you should consult in case you need to make hard decisions such as evictions, raising the rent, and anything that may be grounds for legal action if one wrong move is made.

There are local, state, and federal landlord-tenant laws that you'll need to familiarize yourself with. You should know enough to know what is right and what is wrong.

5. Make sure the property is maintained regularly

This cannot be stressed enough. A well-maintained property will keep the tenants happy. And it will make it more attractive for those who want to fulfill a vacancy.

When there are repairs that need to be done, they need to be done promptly. The tenant and the property manager (be that you or someone else) need to be in communication when the need arises (yes, even at 2 in the morning).

6. Perform regular inspections

Of course, having regular inspections done will keep you ahead of the curve. Especially when you want to avoid disasters from happening. During an inspection, you may find something that may be a minor issue that cannot be ignored.

The sooner you address the issue with some minor maintenance, the better. If they go ignored, then it becomes an even greater problem. At the same time, you want to inspect the properties to ensure that the tenants are following the rules and policies.

7. Prep for tax season

As a property manager, you'll want to prepare for tax season and at least be ahead of the curve. When you have a number of properties, you'll have property managers send you the pertinent documents that you will need to use for tax purposes (when the time comes to file). If you have multiple property managers, the tax prep is a lot easier.

8. Talk to other rental investors

With a network of rental investors that you can easily access, you can be able to get ideas from them in terms of managing their properties. What's been working for them? What hasn't been working?

These investors aren't your competition to the point where you want to put them out of business. These are the kind of people who will help you out whenever you are stuck with something or have a question.

Opting For Property Management

Truth be told, self-managing your property isn't always for everyone. Therefore, you might find that property management is the best option. Even if it's just for one property, having someone else handle the day-to-day operations just might be the best course of action.

Now, let's take a look at the pros and cons of property management so you can make the decision as far as whether or not it becomes the best option:

Pros of property management

- **They have more experience:** Obviously, those who are in property management whether they are an individual or part of a company have the experience. They have the know-how to handle the day-to-day tasks of property management. This includes selecting tenants, handling requests from said tenants, and also coordinating with contractors should any kind of repairs and renovation needs arise.

- **More time on your hands:** Since you will be removing yourself from the day-to-day operations, you'll have more free time on your hands. What you do with it is all up to you. You can still collect the money from all of your properties and be able to use it as you please. The stress will be even less. And you will only be needed in case of emergencies.

- **The response times are quicker:** Yes, the response times will be quicker when you have a property manager on site. When a tenant has an issue with the property such as a broken pipe or the like, the repairman will be there in a jiffy.

- **Vacancies are shorter:** If there is a vacancy, then it won't be long until it's fulfilled. That's because property managers always have a pool of tenants that are available to move into a new place. So they'll screen the applicants and be able to choose the right tenants quickly. On top of that, property management will also have the know-how to retain tenants for the long-term.

Cons of property management

- **It's an additional expense:** Sure, having someone else manage the property will require you to set some money off to the side. Typically, it'll be 10 percent of your monthly income. For example, if your total monthly income for one property is $2000, then $200 will go towards property management. The property management company will earn 10 percent per property that they manage. So if you own five rental properties and the same management company does the day to day operations, that's $1000 a month in total.

- **Communication is needed:** Yes, it's a necessary evil. But you have to be in contact with your property managers on a regular basis. That's because the property you own is still your baby. And you want to know if it's still in good shape. The more you communicate with your property management team, the more peace of mind you'll be knowing that the property is in good hands.

What Should You Ask When Hiring People For Property Management

No smart rental investor will be flying blind when it comes to choosing a property management company to do the day-to-day operations. They need to ask questions that will screen the quality property managers from those who may not do such a good job.

However, there may come a time when they need to make a tough decision because the candidates are highly qualified and bring a lot to the table. So what are the questions you should ask when hiring people for property management? Let's take a look at the following:

Do they hold a license for property management?

Depending on the state you live in, there usually is a license that is required for property management. If they hold a license or have some kind of certification, then there's a good chance you'll place a good amount of trust in them.

What services do you offer?

When it comes to property management, they will usually offer a wide variety of services. Some will usually do leasing and managing. While others go a little further than that.

They may have a wide variety of services such as their own in-house groundskeepers and maintenance crew. If they have that available, that just might be a major plus rather than having to find separate people to handle such tasks. However, that could mean that they'll command higher fees just for the extra services.

How many properties do you currently manage?

This is a key indicator to see how small or large the management business is. This will also give you a look at their current workload. If the property manager is responsible for more than 100 properties, be careful.

If they are handling that many properties, that may mean that they could be paying less attention to some of the properties they are already managing themselves. As a supplemental question, consider asking what kind of properties they normally manage. That way, you'll be more aware of the experience they have.

What are the management fees?

The management fees will be based on the services offered. If the fees exceed 12 to 14 percent of your monthly revenues, then you may want to consider other options. Higher than average fees are fine if they include services that are needed like repairs and maintenance.

Keep in mind that not every management company will offer a fixed monthly fee. Some have different packages at different price points.

How do you decide on rent?

The rent amount may come down to what the property manager thinks is best. They will analyze the market analysis while comparing your property to others. So they may suggest a higher rental rate compared to what you desire. Or it might be lower than what you're gunning for because it might be too high on your end.

How do you screen prospective tenants?

Screening prospective tenants is definitely something that needs to be addressed. So how will a property management go about screening them? Will they look for criminal records?

What about work history? Or perhaps run a background check? This will depend on the kind of tenants you want on your property.

You have a criteria and you want to make sure that it's being followed to a T.

What's the cancellation policy?

If you are looking to sign a contract for a property manager, it's important to know the details. This includes the cancellation policy. Sometimes, things may not work out between you and the property management company.

So it would be incumbent upon you to make the final decision in terms of the contract. You want to cancel at some point if you are not happy with the service. If the terms and conditions are created to keep you tied to each other forever, then that should be a disqualifier (no exceptions).

Do they have references and sample documents?

If the prospective property manager has been doing this for a while, then you want to check with their references. You'll get a good idea of how well they treat their clients. Also, sample documents such as rental leases, applications, financial reports, and even communication between the tenants are highly recommended.

Final Thoughts

Choosing a property manager can be a tough task. But so will managing the property yourself. So it's up to you to make the decision on who will manage the property.

Be sure to carefully weigh the pros and cons. What are you willing to do in terms of property management? What will work best for you?

You may have the time to manage one property and that alone. However, the rest of the properties you own can be managed by a company. In short, make it easier on yourself.

If you are investing in properties and want to sit back and collect some cold hard cash, then a property manager is the way to go. Sure, there is the additional expense. But it's less stress on your part.

Chapter 12 - Agreement: What Should You Include Here?

Now comes the part where you and the tenant will be working out an agreement on the lease. The question that is always asked is what kind of terms must be included? We'll discuss this in more detail as we move farther along in the chapter.

The agreement that you want to put together must be fair and reasonable. It should benefit both you and the tenant. There are important terms that you want to include (and you never want to leave them out either). Once the tenant signs on the dotted line, it's a done deal.

But you want to make sure that all the wrinkles are ironed out first. And the agreement has to be in writing. There are things that you can and cannot do (and the same goes for the tenant). Ensuring that it's all on paper will be one of the most important steps you take as a rental property investor.

If you are ready to go in-depth about how rental agreements would and how you can hammer one out right from the start, keep reading. Let's discuss about protections for yourself and your tenants:

Protecting Yourself And Your Tenant

A written agreement between you and a tenant is obviously one of the most important documents between the two of you. Things can go sideways and it may cause headaches for you or even the tenant themselves. That's why having a binding, written agreement is pretty much required when you are renting out properties.

That's because the tenant may do something that may be prohibited from the agreement. Or you may be doing something that goes beyond the boundaries. Either way, the agreement is designed to keep you both in check.

As far as other types of agreements go, a verbal agreement or even a handshake will never hold up in a court of law. You want physical, written proof just in case the agreement does get contested in a legal setting. You have a document with both yours and the tenant's signature.

If you seem to have any issues with putting together a lease agreement, you may want to consider talking over such terms and conditions with an attorney (assuming you plan on self-managing). If you are handing over the reigns of property management to a property management company, chances are they'll already have a pre-written agreement drawn up.

One of the most important things you'll want to consider when meeting with a property management company before signing them is getting a look at their agreements. You want to find a property manager that can provide a lease agreement that is both fair and balanced for you and the tenant.

What kind of terms should be included? We'll discuss that in a later section. But the point is that the lease agreement must be balanced rather than lop-sided to favor one party or the other.

Two Types Of Agreements

Rental and lease agreements are two types of separate agreements. So it's important to know the difference between the two. We will explain what differs between these two agreements so you are able to draw up the right one for you and your tenant.

There are various items that you want to be aware of in any type of agreement. Before you have a tenant provide you with their signature, here's what you need to know:

Rental agreements

A rental agreement does have similarities to a lease. The most distinguishable difference is the length. The rental agreement will be perfect for shorter periods of time.

If the renter is planning on staying for at least 30 days max, then a rental agreement will be used. Rental agreements will usually be considered on a month-to-month basis. However, the tenant or the landlord can consider making changes if the need arises.

As for the agreement itself, the landlord and the tenant can change the terms of the agreement when the time comes to renew. However, advanced notice should be issued before a new agreement is drawn up.

The pros of a rental agreement will allow more flexibility for the tenant. And the terms can be changed once the old agreement expires and prior to a new one taking place. This will give you and your tenant time to discuss some potential changes.

The downsides of this will basically be on your end. You may deal with a frequent turnover rate. Furthermore, it can also make your rental income stream very unpredictable.

Lease agreements

So as you've figured out by now, the lease agreements pertain to the long-term. Most lease agreements will last anywhere between 6 to 12 months. This will allow the tenant to live on the property for a fixed period of time.

The lease is drawn up using clear and thorough terms that both the landlord and the tenant must understand. The agreement must also include a set of rules, the duration of the agreement, the rental rate, and other terms and conditions. It is important for you to have your prospective tenants look over the lease agreement before it is signed.

You want to give them a chance to solidify their decision and at least allow them to ask questions or address concerns regarding the lease agreement itself. This lease agreement must be organized, well thought-out, and well-written so that both parties have a clear understanding and be aware that they are both protected.

The agreement cannot be altered or changed for the duration of the lease. So the lease must be honored by both parties. Any breach or violation can lead to a legal situation that neither you nor your tenant want to get into.

The pros of a lease include a structured long-term agreement. The occupancy will be stable at best. For these reasons, you will also get a predictable stream of income.

The cons of this are that the rental costs will stay the same for the life of the lease. This means you won't be able to raise the rent rate while the space is being occupied. Lastly, you could lose out on incremental gains of income should the market value increase.

10 Important Terms To Include

Now, it's time to consider what kind of terms that you want to include in the agreement. You don't have to be a legal expert to know what to put in one. However, you'd be smart to have it reviewed by an attorney before it is even signed by both you and the tenant.

But for the time being, let's focus on the important terms that you want to put in. These are items that you also don't want to omit from any agreement. Once these terms are included, you can make some changes (but not get rid of the terms altogether).

Here are the ten key terms you want to include in your agreements:

1. The names of all tenants and occupants

Who is going to reside on the property? This should include members of couples who are married or unmarried. Any adults living on the property even as roommates must be included in the agreement.

The reason why all adults must be included is due to the fact that it provides you with additional insurance. Each tenant must be responsible for paying the monthly rent in full and follow all terms of the agreement itself. Also, it puts you in a position where you can seek out rent from the other occupants if one tenant fails to pay it.

Also, if one tenant violates an agreement, you can terminate the tenancy of that tenant or all of them. That decision is entirely up to you. But you'd be more apt to remove the violator rather than the rest of the tenants who may be among the innocent party.

An occupancy clause should also be included so that you can put in writing that only tenants or any of their dependents (i.e -- minor children) can live in the rental. You can also include a clause regarding how long guests can stay. You also can include in the clause regarding sublets or new tenants.

Any new tenants or persons subletting must be notified by you in advance. Failure to do so can provide you with enough power to terminate the tenancy and evict the offending resident (or all residents).

2. Description of the property

The information of the property must include the physical address. If it is an apartment building, it should also include the building and the unit number. Also, take into account the number of parking spaces and storage areas it has.

If there is an assigned parking space for an apartment unit, be sure to have that mentioned in the agreement itself. For example, if the tenant is living in Building 1, Apartment A then the parking space marked as 'B1A' or the like should be provided. The same will go for any storage space.

Meanwhile, you should also include in the agreement any areas of the property that the tenant can or cannot have access to. If you have a locked shed in the backyard of one of the apartment buildings, you'll have to include in the agreement whether or not that can be accessed by the tenant.

If the shed cannot be accessible by the tenants, make sure you have a notice saying so on the shed itself. You'll want to cover as many bases as possible without it looking like overkill.

3. Time Period Of Tenancy

Pretty self-explanatory. If it's a rental agreement, usually it's a 30 day agreement. If it's a lease, then it can be anywhere between six months to a year. Month-to-month or one fixed date (i.e January 1, 2021 to January 1, 2022), it should be addressed in this part of the agreement.

Be sure to take note of the start date, how long the tenancy length will be, and when the lease will expire.

4. Rental rate

The rental rate will vary from one agreement to the next (assuming it's a rental agreement). A lease agreement will have one rental rate that will stay the same for the life of the lease. Meanwhile, don't stop with just a numerical figure.

The payment terms must include how a tenant can pay. Will cash be accepted? Will they be able to pay the rent via check, credit card, wire transfer, etc.?

Consider the payment acceptance options and get a good idea of how a tenant wants to pay you. Also, you should consider the idea of charging a late fee should a tenant miss a rent payment. You may want to consider a grace period (and the conditions that will allow a tenant to qualify).

You should consider additional charges if a rent check bounces. The state and local rent laws should be consulted upon while you are working on putting together this part of the agreement. There are laws that may allow or disallow how a tenant must pay the landlord (such as by mail).

5. Security Deposits and Fees

Typically, a security deposit and any additional fees must be included in the agreement. One thing to be sure of is to take a look at the security deposit limit laws in your state. Typically, a security deposit will usually equal out to the same amount of money compared to your rental rate. For example, if the rent is $1000 a month then the security deposit can be $1000.

It's also important to determine how the security deposit will be used. The purpose of the security deposit will usually cover any unpaid rent or any repairs stemming from damage caused by the tenants themselves. It may not be accepted in lieu of rent payment for the previous month.

You can also determine whether or not you want the tenant to replenish the security deposit should there be a mid-tenancy deduction. Also, you want to lay out the terms on how the security deposit will be returned once the tenant moves out.

Lastly, let's take a look at the fees. What kind of fees will be included in the agreement? For example, you could have a tenant that will move in with a pet.

The fees can vary on how you set it. It can be a flat fee or it can depend on the size of a pet. In the event of the latter, you could charge a lesser pet fee for someone who may have a chihuahua compared to a tenant who may have a larger breed. Also, if you are planning on implementing non-refundable fees, then consider taking a look at any state laws that allow such fees in the first place.

6. Policies for maintenance and repairs

When it comes to the stress that comes with rent-withholdings or security deposit disputes, a repair and maintenance policy will definitely come in handy. The policy should outline what the tenant should be responsible for. For example, the tenant must be responsible for keeping the property clean and in good condition.

It may also be the responsibility of the tenant to alert you of any conditions that are considered unsafe or unsanitary. You should also outline any procedures that the tenants must follow should such things arise. Also, you may allow or disallow what a tenant can do in terms of any repairs or maintenance (i.e -- allowing them to paint one of the rooms or not).

7. The right to enter the rental property

Yes, it's your property. And it's clear that your tenant deserves the right to privacy. It's important to make sure that the right to enter the rental property is included in every agreement. You do not want to be accused of illegal entry or invading the privacy of the tenant.

Take a look at the access laws in your state before drawing up this agreement. You can implement a policy for situations like repairs or showing the unit to a new tenant that will occupy it when the outgoing one moves out. You'd be smart to inform the tenants with a 24 hour advance notice that you will be entering the property in the event of repairs or maintenance (or showings). In case of emergency, you may provide advance notice, but it may be less than a 24 hour time frame.

Either way, this is one good reason why communication between you and a tenant must be important.

8. Other rules and policies

What other rules and policies can be included? For example, is smoking allowed on the property? Will you allow pets?

All of this is completely up to you. You should include what is allowed on the property and what is prohibited. Illegal activities like drug use, drug dealing, violating noise ordinances and laws must also be addressed here as well. This will ensure that your property will be safe for other tenants (especially when young children are living on the property).

9. Contact information

Include information on how a tenant must contact you. At the same time, you'll want to keep records of any conversations between you and the tenant. This can include text messages, instant messages, phone calls, written communication, and so on.

In the event of some legal occurrences, you can use the communication made between you and the tenant as evidence. This also includes any advanced notices such as entering the property for repairs, maintenance, or showing the property to a new tenant. Make sure that you check your email regularly or any kind of communication so you and your tenant are on the same page.

10. Required disclosures

This term must be in compliance with any federal, state, or local laws (if any). You will need to inform the tenant of any potential issues such as lead paint, the unit's history of any invasive species such as bed bugs, and more. Also, you'll want to make sure that your lease agreement is free of any violations that may be related to anti-discrimination laws, rent control laws, or any health and safety codes outlined by the government.

The Signing Process of the Agreement

So now, the ink will go to the paper. However, the question is: who signs first? Let's take a look at the step-by-step process of the agreement and the signing process:

1. Make sure all parties are involved

If there is one tenant and you, then get to signing it. If there are multiple tenants or adult occupants, make sure that all are present before the agreement is signed. You must have all signatures on the document before the agreement is finalized.

2. The tenants sign first

Tying it into the previous step, all tenants who are occupying the property must sign the agreement first. Once the tenant's signature is on the dotted line, you can advance to the following step.

3. You or the property manager can sign it

The agreement can be signed by you or the property manager that is deferred to handle the process. Once it is signed on yours or the manager's end, be sure to have copies prepared for both yourself, the property manager, and the tenants involved. It's important to have these copies kept in the records in the event of any misunderstandings or potential legal proceedings (should they arise).

Unfortunate Events and How To Deal With Them

On rental properties, the unfortunate things can and will happen. It's important to have a battle plan drawn up so you can make the right decision. Such events can result in a tenant getting evicted and the agreement being terminated in accordance to your terms.

Is it possible that a tenant can break a lease agreement before they even move in? What happens if they break the lease itself? What will be your decision going forward?

Things do happen to where it might send you scrambling for answers. For example, a tenant can change their mind at the last minute about moving into one of your rental properties. Or there may be various circumstances that can happen to where a move in cannot occur.

Let's take a look at the various situations:

When a tenant breaks a lease before moving in?

This can occur in events that a tenant may have no control over. They can include but are not limited to job transfers or family emergencies. However, a prospective tenant may also have cold feet over the idea of moving into the property.

This is where things can get really tricky. But it's up to you to make the right decision. However, there needs to be documentation present.

It is yours or the property manager's responsibility to document everything including any early termination letters. In the event if something goes to court, you'll have these to fall back on. The question that needs to be answered is whether or not there are legal obligations that need to be fulfilled should a tenant break a lease before moving in.

Consider the following:

Advanced Notice

If a tenant is breaking a lease before moving in, you want to request a written notice. This should be done at least 30 days before the tenant's scheduled move in. The tenant must notify you or the landlord that the lease will be broken.

Inform them of the next steps

From there, you can notify the tenant that they are legally liable for paying the rent for the duration of the agreement. However, you will inform the tenant that you will also re-rent the property in accordance with any good faith efforts that are required by state law (depending on the state).

Once the property is rented out again, the previous tenant can no longer pay rent on the property. But in the meantime, they must do so whether they occupy the property or not.

Find a new tenant

As part of the good faith efforts, you must find a new tenant. Start by marketing your vacancy as soon as possible and have the new tenant sign a lease agreement quickly. This way, the old tenant can no longer have the burden of paying rent on a property that they do not occupy.

What is the standard protocol?

The standard protocol in this situation includes the following:

- Requesting an early termination letter

- Explaining that the tenant is responsible for the rent while you search for a new tenant

- Collecting rent once the new tenant has agreed to a lease (or applied the security deposit)

Also, you have the option of retaining the security deposit if the lease is broken before a tenant moves in. This will cover any losses that may have been accrued due to this early termination. Remember to consult your state and local laws regarding security deposits before determining whether or not you should keep the security deposit.

When a tenant breaks a lease with advanced notice

In the event of this occurrence, use the same standard protocol above. On top of that, it's important to communicate with your tenant to get a good timeline of when that tenant will vacate the property. Be sure they give you as much advance notice as possible.

This will allow you enough time to find a new tenant so the outgoing tenant may not be stuck with paying the rent for the duration of the lease. Fill the vacancy as soon as possible. And go about fulfilling the screening process like you normally do when finding a new tenant.

When a lease is broken without notice

You may have a tenant that can vacate the property without giving you any notice whatsoever. Especially when they knowingly do so. People can be quite inconsiderate.

This kind of occurrence is not uncommon. And there's a good chance that this will happen to you more than once (usually on an occasional basis). While finding a new tenant, try to find the former tenant and explain to them the situation.

You may consider legal action if necessary. If you breach a rental agreement or lease, then that will allow the tenant to end the agreement itself before the expiration date. The tenant will not be subject to any penalties or legal trouble because the lease was already broken by you in the first place.

Keep in mind that if there are any violations to the agreement, you can invoke the right to terminate the tenancy and evict the tenant depending on the violation itself. For example, if the police have discovered that a tenant is dealing drugs on the property, they will notify you. From there, you can evict the tenant.

Final Thoughts

The agreement between you and the tenant must be a sacred document. Both of you must sign the agreement and pledge to honor it for as long as it's in effect. When the agreement expires, that's when you and the tenant(s) can renew it.

When the time comes to renew an agreement, you can consider exchanging ideas with the tenants on what could be included (and they can suggest some ideas as well). This could mean a possible bump up in rent (or even a reduction). Or the tenant may want something that the landlord may be willing to allow.

You should have a good idea of what to include in the agreement. That way, if something ever gets challenged to the point where it's a legal issue, that agreement will be a good piece of evidence. An ironclad agreement will help keep you and your tenant(s) in check.

Chapter 13 - Let's Talk About Your Tenants

Your tenants are the lifeblood to any rental property. Without them, the property doesn't generate income. And you don't get the return on investment that you want.

Sounds simple enough, doesn't it? With that said, we're going to talk about how you want to find the right kind of tenant. We'll even give you the definition of a good tenant and how you can find them.

We'll also walk you through the application process so you know what the tenant will need to fill out and how the application will be viewed by you or the property manager. We'll also be taking a look at five different kinds of tenants that you need to keep an eye on.Finally, we'll also discuss how you should deal with difficult tenants.

As a property manager, you want to work with tenants who are reasonable, easy to get along with, and are known to not cause all kinds of trouble. Not only that, you'll want to consider the health and safety of your other tenants. One bad tenant may cause trouble for your property (or even the neighborhood itself).

If you are serious about finding the right kind of tenants, this chapter will be your go-to guide on how to fulfill your vacancies with them. Let's dive right in:

Defining a Good Tenant

The question on every property owner's mind is what makes a great tenant? We'll be taking a look at some of the characteristics that makes one stand a head above shoulders over the rest. You'd be hard-pressed to find a good tenant that will have these attributes that we'll be listing below.

You want to keep this list handy especially if you are putting together a series of screening questions while looking through their application. The more they fit your criteria, the better off they will be. Here are the following things that define a great tenant:

Their credit history

A good credit history is a green flag. You know that they are in good financial standing. And they will be reliable when it comes time to pay the rent.

Granted, you will know for a fact that they will be financially responsible for as long as they are a tenant (be it for the short-term or long-term). If their credit is not the best, then that may be a cause for concern. For others, it might be automatic denial.

This decision to approve or deny a tenant based on their credit history should be all up to you.

Income

Proof of income is one more good indicator that you will find a tenant that is financially stable and able to pay monthly rent. A good steady income is what the ideal tenant will have in order to qualify to become a tenant. If their income is roughly three times the monthly rent (i.e -- if the rent is $1,000 a month, their income must be $3,000 a month) then that's a good sign.

Remember to factor in any debt that they may also have. If they have a high level of debt, that's typically a red flag that you want to pay attention to. Even if they have the income to pay monthly rent, the debt may be too great to bear yet another expense.

Criminal background

If you want an apartment building that is safe for all tenants, then a criminal background check is a must.

This should go the same way for single-family properties. A lack of a criminal record is obviously a plus.

Criminal information is public record, so you can obtain it somewhere however you wish. Your property management company may also have access to resources where they can perform background checks including criminal records. But what about the crimes themselves?

Various misdemeanor crimes may not be grounds for automatic rejection. But there may be some violent crimes that will also not be tolerated as well. Also, you may be faced with the difficult task of dealing with a tenant who may be a registered sex offender.

The cleaner a tenant's criminal record, the better. But if there are any crimes that they are convicted of, sometimes you should consider asking them for an explanation. At the end of the day, who would you want to occupy your property?

Rental history

The tenant's rental history is usually a good indicator of what kind of a tenant that you are going to deal with. This will allow you to contact past landlords and ask them questions about the tenant who wants to move into your property.

If you hear nothing but positive things about them, then that's a good sign. And that should put the prospective tenant at the top of your list. You'll find out information about how good of a tenant they were, why they moved out, and if they honored tenant agreements.

Respect

A tenant that respects you is someone who will not take advantage of you. And they won't play games with you whenever they miss a payment or are about to. They also will take great care of the property itself.

Those who have damaged the property or play games with the landlords will usually be the ones that lack respect. They may not respect your time, nor will they care about the fact that you are trying to run a business. And they will always make excuses when things go wrong and they try to avoid fault from it.

Honesty

You want a tenant that is honest. You want a tenant that is transparent. And you want a tenant that will be upfront with you.

Therefore, it is important to find a tenant that is someone you can trust. A good honest tenant will protect the property and hold themselves accountable whenever they damage something. Trust goes a long way (and it's a two-way street).

You and your tenant should build a trusting relationship that lasts well beyond the time when the tenant leaves the property and relocates elsewhere. That in turn gives you the opportunity to put in a good word for them whenever they decide to rent another property or buy a home.

Cleanliness

You want a tenant that will keep the property in good condition. So cleanliness is a must. You might have heard plenty of horror stories about tenants leaving a property without warning.

And when the landlord comes to check on it, the floors are covered in trash and a place is an absolute mess. You can feel your skin crawl just thinking about it. To avoid that from ever happening, you'll want to refer to other landlords that rented from this tenant.

How was the property when the tenant moved out? Was it clean? Did it pass any inspections?

If you see the tenant in person, how do they look? If you walk them to their car, how does the inside look? There are some things you need to look for to determine whether or not they will keep the property clean or not.

Are they prepared for the worst?

Will they alert you if there is anything bad that is happening like a burst pipe or a fire? Will they purchase renter's insurance if things go wrong? These are questions that you might be considering to determine whether or not they are prepared for what may be the worst that can happen on a property.

How To Find Good Tenants

Now that you have a good idea on which characteristics to look for in a tenant, it's time to find them. It's not easy finding tenants that will pay on time, be respectful, and able to stick around for the long haul. Knowing where to find them will be key.

There are tenants that work in different industries, come from different walks of life, and so on. Are you looking for tenants who work in professional fields? Are the tenants you seek out students?

There are many tenants out there that have well-paying jobs. And some are usually working minimum wage jobs, but can afford an apartment or split the rent with a roommate or their significant other. Here are some ways to find a good tenant:

Know where to advertise

If you are in search of a new tenant, it's important to know where to advertise. What are the local newspapers in your area? What about groups on social media that are tailored to your local area?

Why not rely on digital advertising? What kind of tenants do you want to attract? Where do those ideal tenants like to 'hang out' all the time?

You can advertise using social media, print ads, or even print flyers on a bulletin board. Either way, you'll want to let people know that there is a vacancy on your property that has yet to be fulfilled. And it's available to any tenant who can be able to fulfill the requirements.

Be sure to include the location, how prospective tenants can contact you, and include the amenities and what's included (if applicable). You want to disclose as much information about the property as possible as it might be the perfect property for your tenant to live in.

Post good photographs of the property

Whether it's online or on the flyer, you want to take good photographs of the property. You want it to be attractive and appealing to the prospective tenant. Also, make sure that the property is clean and free of any damage.

Be transparent

When a prospective tenant wants to know more about you and your properties, they will usually do some research themselves. They will find out reviews about you as a landlord and the properties that you have rented out.

If the reviews are more positive than negative, then they may be convinced that you're the kind of landlord that they trust. If there are negative reviews, don't 'scrub' them or delete them just to make yourself look good.

Be honest and transparent as possible. Likewise, you will have tenants who will do the same.

The Application Process

The application process for you and your tenant should be straightforward. On their end, they fill out the specific information such as their name, current employment, proof of income, and references. On your end, you want to check to see if they gave you the right information so the background checks and the like are quick and easy to do.

Also, you want to avoid some kind of interview process. You may not have time to interview everyone and prospective tenants may be turned off by the idea of being interviewed for a place to live. So avoid that at all possible.

Here are some other tips to keep in mind of when you are going through the application process:

Check their credit history

Again, this will give you an indication of whether or not they are reliable for payments. The better their credit score, the more likely they will pay you on time without any issue.

Check their income

Same reason as above. You want their income to be stable and predictable. Remember, if it's three times the rent price, that's a good sign.

But don't forget, they also may have debts that are paying off. If the debts are manageable, then don't

249

worry about it. If they seem to be piling up, then you may want to consider other tenant applications.

A criminal background check is a must

When it comes to your property, you want to make sure that your tenant is someone that is not a threat to themselves or anyone's safety. Conduct a background check and see if they have a clean criminal record. You may want to consider avoiding those who have been previously convicted for crimes like drug crimes, sexually based crimes like rape, sexual assault, etc., or even domestic violence.

However, this is based on your own discretion. Decide where you draw the line in terms of which crimes are not grounds for disqualification.

Eviction history

Has the prospective tenant been evicted before? And if so, how many times. The more times they have been evicted, the less likely that tenant will fulfill your vacancy.

It may seem like a no brainer just to reject their application.

Keep Watch Against These Five Tenants

The last thing you want is to deal with tenants who are going to be a headache. Lucky for you, we've been able to provide you a list of the types of tenants that should not even be on your property. During the screening process or even showing them the property, you'll want to get a good idea of whether or not these are one of the five types of tenants you want to avoid or not.

Enough talk, let's get to the good stuff and inform you on who to potentially avoid:

Those that don't pay on time

Let's face it, there are those who will miss a rental payment from time to time due to sudden expenses. And that's where a good grace period comes in handy. But what if they don't pay on time habitually?

That's going to become a problem. So it would make sense to reject a tenant who has a repeated history of paying rent late or never at all. You want predictable, reliable streams of income and this kind of tenant does not provide that.

To avoid this kind of tenant, a simple credit check will do the trick. That way, you'll know whether or not they are caught up on their payments or if they are drowning in debt.

Tenants that damage the property

You already have enough repairs and maintenance to deal with. So extra damage should be the last thing you want to deal with. Not to mention, it can cause an overrun in your repair expenses.

This is where a background check comes in handy. You can also check out their rental history. From there, you can ask landlords how that tenant took care of the property. If they say that they have damaged the place on a regular basis, then that's grounds for an automatic rejection.

The tenants that refuse to leave

Ah yes, they have broken the lease or have failed to pay. But when the time comes to evict them, they refuse to leave the property. In some cases, they may need to be forcibly removed by law enforcement.

To avoid this nightmare from happening, refer to the background checks. Also, see if there were any past landlords that had to deal with such an issue with the specific tenant you are looking at. If the residence history on their application is lacking information, then that may be a red flag (but that's where other references come into play).

The bothersome tenants

These are the people who make a lot of noise, have strange odors coming from the unit, or they are just rude and obnoxious people that are being a nuisance to the other tenants. If they have a history of upsetting their neighbors, including them on your property could crank up the tenant turnover rate.

Again, this is the perfect reason why you should always ask past landlords or even references about any behavioral issues a tenant may have. If they are not bothersome in the slightest, that's a green light to move forward.

The 'sue happy' tenants

These tenants are going to be a problem. And there's a good reason why you want to consult with past landlords. These tenants will always find something to argue about with you and then try and find a way to drag you to court.

If this tenant has applied to occupy your vacancy and they tend to bring other landlords to court because of some odd reason, do not for a single second approve their application or look at it any further.

Difficult Tenants: How Should You Deal With Them?

Granted, the best time to deal with difficult tenants is before you even approve or reject their application. However, what if the background checks and everything else go well without a hitch? What if the nightmare begins well after the fact?

In this section, you will now have a proven battle plan on how to deal with tenants who will give you more stress than not. First and foremost, it's important to keep a level head and be able to control yourself emotionally.

Secondly, it's important to know your boundaries as a landlord and know the tenant's boundaries as well. Also, remember that the terms of the agreement are yours and you will exercise them as such. Here are some things to consider when dealing with difficult tenants:

If they don't pay on time

As mentioned before, if they miss a payment but are usually on time then you should consider giving them a grace period to catch up. As a courtesy, you can waive the late fee (if you have one implemented). Sometimes, emergency expenses can happen to a point where they have to postpone a rent payment.

However, the habitual offenders will need to be dealt with accordingly. If they make a late payment, you tack on an extra charge. If they don't pay at all, you have it within your right to evict them in accordance to the lease.

As it is, the tenant agreed to pay on time in accordance to the lease. Therefore, it's technically breaking it if they do not pay on time or refuse to do so.

If they damage the property

Again, things can happen. They can accidentally damage the property and hold themselves responsible. Be sure they have a written copy of a damage report (as should you). You can deduct it from their security deposit or waive the charge if it was a no-fault damage.

But if they continuously damage it to the point where the handyman is spending most of his time on the property, that will also give you the power to evict them. Once again, damaging the property frequently does breach the lease (especially the term to where they agreed to keep the property in good condition).

Those who sublet without prior notification

Subletting is perfectly fine. Unless the tenant notifies you ahead of time and you give them the go ahead. Depending on where you live, subleasing a property is against the law.

If that's the case, you want to make that clear in your agreement with the tenant. It's OK for them to have guests so long as they stay for a few days (but never beyond that). However, no one should have to live on your property without them paying their share of the rent.

The overindulgent pet owner

Pet owners can be a nightmare tenant for one reason or another. Oftentimes, they always respect the rules and boundaries. These are pet owners who allow them to do their business inside the property.

You'd be surprised by how much damage can be caused by pet urine. Not to mention, it can leave quite a smell. You can deal with these tenants by charging them extra for the pet fee.

To prevent this from happening from the beginning, then you'll want to establish a strict 'no pets' policy on your property. But evicting them from the property will be difficult since they may not have any other place to go with their pets.

And if you love your pets, it would be very hard to get rid of them. Or, you can persuade the tenant to have them rehomed with a member of their family or a friend.

The ones that won't leave

If they are being evicted and refuse to leave, then you contact law enforcement. However, you can't kick out a tenant while the lease is still valid either. An eviction can be done as a last resort or if the tenant has engaged in illegal activities.

However, you'll want to go through the proper legal channels to ensure you are not violating the lease or any kind of laws.

Lawbreakers

If a tenant is breaking the law on your property, the best move is to call the police. They will deal with the situation from there. Drug sales and violence will always need to be dealt with by law enforcement.

As such, you can prevent this from happening just by simply doing background checks. A criminal history could be the difference between a reliable tenant and a difficult one.

Final Thoughts

Finding the right tenant is all part of the process. That's why you need to screen each applicant (or have your property manager do the screening). You have an idea of what your perfect tenant should be.

For one, they are reliable when it comes to payments. Second, they are honest and transparent. And finally, they are willing to respect the rules and be a good tenant (and a good neighbor as well).

Also, it's better to catch on early to avoid dealing with one of the five types of tenants we've listed above. If one of them seems to 'fall through the cracks' after awhile, that's when you'll need to take matters into your own hands if needed.

Remember, you must also follow the laws to ensure that you are not taking an unjust action against a tenant. No matter how much of a pain they can be, you can find a way to deal with them. Even if you have to go through the legal channels, it can be done.

However, doing a thorough screening that includes a background check is something that you or a property manager should be doing all the time when reviewing tenant applications. It's a decision that can mean more cash flow or less.

Chapter 14 - Before, During, and After Renting Out Your Property

In this chapter, we'll be guiding you through the process on what you'll need to do before, during, and after renting out your property to a tenant. It's always a good idea to know that the property is in good shape and is ready for a tenant to occupy once everything looks good. The last thing you want is a tenant to move in one second and then call you the next after experiencing a myriad of issues.

We'll be discussing why preparing the property for tenants will be essential. And we'll also talk about how to go about doing a walk-through and inspection. This is where you really need to pay attention to detail here.

Also, it would be a good idea to consider the idea of insurance coverage and determine the kind of policy you want. We'll discuss insurance policies in depth and what can be covered by them. Finally, we'll discuss maintenance and repairs and everything you need to know about them.

As you are about to rent out your first ever rental property, it's good to know these things so you have happy tenants. Not only that, you want to keep your expenses to a minimum. The last thing you want is to be throwing money out the window due to constant costs with repairs and maintenance.

Let's keep going and talk about what to do before renting out the property:

Preparing The Rental Property For Tenants

Preparing the rental property will require you to make sure that everything is clean and in good condition. But that doesn't stop there. Here are some of the other things that you need to do when preparing for tenants:

- **Check for phone and Internet connections:** These days, many people rely on their smartphones. However, there are still those that rely on a landline. See if there are appropriate setups for phone and Internet. If WiFi is included in the rent, make sure that it's set up properly and the tenant is able to connect once they move in.

- **Test the HVAC and plumbing:** You want to make sure that things are in working order. Test the plumbing by running the sinks or even flushing the toilet. Also, see if the HVAC system is running properly. Is the place heating up good?

- **Are there curtains for privacy:** Privacy matters most to a tenant. So it's better to make sure there are curtains set up in appropriate places. Blinds and shades are acceptable as well.

- **Make sure there are smoke detectors:** There should be an unwritten rule that all of your rental properties must have working smoke detectors. Safety is paramount for your tenants. Have smoke detectors set up in the kitchen, bedrooms, or any place that is appropriate.

- **Are the locks working properly:** Security should be just as important as safety. Check the locks on entryway doors and ensure that they are working properly. A failing lock or a door that doesn't lock can be quite the goldmine for those who want to break in and steal valuables.

- **Make sure that everything is clean:** How are the rugs? Is everything mopped and swept? Did you wipe down the sinks? Everything must be clean or even spotless before the tenant even sets foot on the property.

- **Complete repairs and maintenance tasks if needed:** If there is something broken, fix it. If there is something that needs cleaning, clean it. You'll want to see if the appliances are in working order and are not faulty. Make sure everything else isn't faulty or in need of repairs.

- **Don't forget the outdoors:** Preparation isn't just for the indoors. Make sure that the front and back yards are clean, the lawn is mowed, and the property looks like it's in good condition. Clear the front entryway of any cobwebs. Make sure the driveway is nice and clean.

Doing A Walk-Through and Inspection

This is a task that you absolutely, positively gotta do. Especially when you are steps away from handing over the keys to a tenant. Because you want to make sure everything is running smoothly.

Not only that, you want to see if the structure of the property is in good enough shape rather than crumbling and falling apart. Inspections should occur not just before a tenant moves in, but during the time when a tenant is occupying the property and after they move out. In the event of the 'during', you want to give your tenants advanced notice (and

263

make sure that the tenants themselves acknowledge it).

When you do a move out inspection, it will help you determine if there are any repair costs that may incur. The inspection could yield no need for repairs or just a few tweaks and adjustments, if necessary. If there are repairs needed, then it may be the responsibility of the tenant to get it fixed before they move out.

This will also determine whether or not if the tenant will get the full security deposit back or part of it. If there are some damages that need to be fixed, it can be taken out of the deposit itself before the rest is handed back to the outgoing tenant. At the same time, these inspections are important so they minimize the amount of disputes between the landlord and the outgoing tenant.

Both you and the tenant should each do an inspection of what's in good shape and what needs repairing. This includes inspecting every room. Check the floors, walls, ceilings, light fixtures, closest, and everything else. If there are repairs that need to be done, you or the tenant will need to get an estimation of how much it will cost (assuming one or the other decides to repair it).

Before the move-in

If your tenant is in the process of moving in, consider doing a pre-move in walkthrough and inspection. Again, this will help you double check whether or not things are in working order. Things can happen between the last inspection and the pre-move in inspection, so you want to make sure your bases are covered.

As mentioned before, check every room. See if the plumbing system is running properly. Test the HVAC, smoke detectors, and locks to ensure if they are working properly. If things are working properly, that's an all-clear for the tenant to move in.

Also, you should have the tenant on site while the both of you are doing a walkthrough. That way, the both of you can confirm that things are in good working order. And it can give the tenant peace of mind knowing that they are moving into a place that isn't falling apart.

Damage can happen even before you and the tenant set foot on the property. So it's better to do the walk-through together. The tenant will most likely not be at fault for such damage, so it's better to take their word for it (especially when the damage is minor).

Insurance Coverage Needs Some Adjustments

Insurance coverage for your property is designed to protect your property from certain dangers, disasters, and damages. You'd be wise to have it on every piece of property you own. Having an ironclad insurance policy is key whether you own one rental property or several.

Also, it's important to remind your tenants that your insurance policy is different. If something happens to the property, it does not cover and damage that occurs to a tenant's possessions. Therefore, you'll want to let them know about renter's insurance.

Renter's insurance will cover the tenant in the event of things happening on the property. So while your property gets damaged due to the fire and your tenant loses everything, the both of you should have peace of mind knowing that you're both covered under property and renter's insurance respectively. You should also look for a rental insurance company that you can recommend to your tenants while the two of you are discussing things about the property itself.

One of your number one goals is to keep the tenants happy. So giving them valuable information like renter's insurance and how important it is to them is a good idea. Your tenants should be a priority to you and taking good care of them is all they ask for.

Remember, there are different insurance policies that cover specific properties. For example, if your property is a long-term rental, make sure that you find an insurance policy that covers them. Likewise, there are insurance plans that are aimed towards properties that are considered short-term rentals.

There may also be requirements that you need to fulfill prior to covering your property. For example, if it's a long-term rental, then you'll want to make sure there's a landlord or rental dwelling insurance policy that is available. This policy will cover about a quarter more than the usual homeowner's insurance.

These policies will usually cover physical damage to the property caused by fire, lightning, snow, ice, wind, and other natural dangers. Also, find a policy that allows coverage for personal property that is designed for maintenance purposes such as lawn mowers and snow blowers. The policy should also cover tenant appliances such as refrigerators, washers, dryers, and so on.

Everything You Should Know About Maintenance And Repairs

Maintenance and repairs keep the property in good condition. The last thing your tenant wants to do is live in a place that is falling apart completely. In other words, you don't want the place to be a 'death trap'.

As far as repairs and maintenance is concerned, there's often a lot of confusion of who would be responsible for them. The short answer: it depends. For simplicity sake, we can say that if something happens and damage occurs through no fault of the tenant, it shouldn't be their responsibility to repair the damage.

However, it is their responsibility to let you or the property manager know. That way, you or the property manager can contact the right person to deal with the issue at hand. But if the damage is incurred by the tenant (be it accidental or intentional), then there's a good chance that it will be their responsibility to get it repaired at their own expense.

At the same time, they must be aware that such damages and repair expenses can be taken out of their security deposit. That's just the basic structure of how it all should work. But what else should the landlord or the tenant be responsible for?

Let's take a look at the following:

What the landlord or property manager is responsible for:

- **Keeping up with health and building codes:** The best time to ensure that your property is following health and safety codes is before a tenant moves in. The second best time is when the property is occupied and you need to notify the tenant.

- **If there is pest and mold present:** Damage caused by pests or mold are of no fault of the tenant. These things can occur without the knowledge of the tenant. And usually these are discovered when it's later rather than early. Preventative maintenance is important to ensure that pests and mold do not make their presence known on the property.

- **Changing the locks:** It should be the responsibility of the landlord to change locks in between tenants. In fact, there are most states that require this by law. However, if you fail to change the locks, then the tenant will have the legal right to do so on their own accord.

- **Structural integrity and protection against weather:** The property should always be in good shape. You don't want it falling apart or being susceptible to damage when nature decides to unleash something nasty. Make sure that there are no major cracks or broken doors and windows. Any damage that may create an unsafe or uninhabitable condition must be addressed immediately.

- **HVAC and plumbing:** You want to make sure that the heat is available in the winter and air conditioning is present in the summer. You also want to make sure that the water can run cold or hot. Lastly, make sure that the property has power. There are things that can happen to them to where you need to repair them.

What the tenant is responsible for:

- **Trash disposal:** Clearly, the tenant must keep the place clean. Trash must be taken out on a regular basis for pickup. Failure to do so can draw in pests, molds, and odors. Trash service may be covered under the rental agreement as part of the rent or must be paid as a tenant expense.

- **Reporting issues for maintenance:** If something is broken that needs to be fixed (and it's under the landlord's responsibilities), then they must inform the landlord or property manager. The same goes for any damages that the tenant themselves occur. This way, they claim responsibility and will inform the landlord that they will be paid for the repairs and damage.

- **Issues that indicate misuse of property:** To define this, this means that a tenant may be doing something that goes against the lease agreement. For example, if a pet causes damage or if there is damage due to smoking on the property (when the agreement explicitly disallows it).

Final Thoughts

Your rental property is your baby. That can't be said enough. And when someone else is moving in as a tenant, you want to make sure that they are doing their part in keeping it in good shape.

Make sure that inspections are done before, during, and after the property is rented out. Your tenant and yourself (or the property owner) should be in regular communication to ensure that the property is in good condition. If there are issues, you or the property manager must be aware.

You have to make sure that everything is in working order. A pre move-in inspection is necessary so things are working properly and that the right safety precautions are taken (such as installing smoke alarms and properly working locks). Your tenant deserves safety and security in a place they want to call home.

Remember to lay out the boundaries in terms of repairs and maintenance. Have them understand what kind of repairs and maintenance they are responsible for. Meanwhile, let them know of the kind of maintenance and repairs that fall under your responsibilities when something happens.

Also, remind them that it is their responsibility to report and need for maintenance or damage on the property. And they also need renter's insurance to cover the damage or loss of possessions should something happen to the property. Simply put, you and your tenant should be able to have the confidence in knowing that when a problem arises, all of the bases will be covered.

Make this a win-win for both you and your tenants. They want a landlord that they can trust and you want the same out of your ideal tenant.

Now that we've got all of that out of the way, let's talk about your 'exit plan' should you have one.

Chapter 15 - Exit Strategies: What To Do When You Want To Sell Your Rental Properties

If you are planning on purchasing rental properties to generate income for a lifetime, then that's one thing. In fact, that's one of the strategies we'll talk about in this final chapter. But what if you decide that it's time to move on?

We'll be talking about some of the exit strategies that are available to use so that you can be able to cash out after a positive return on investment and then some. Having an exit strategy that is well-thought out and executed properly is your aim here.

When it comes time to sell a property, you do not want to be sloppy about it. You want things to be straightened out, well-organized, and walk away knowing that your now former property is in the right hands. We'll explain what an exit strategy is and what it will take to put one together.

While there are more than a few proven exit strategies out there, we'll be taking a look at the four most common types: the fix and flip, the buy and hold, wholesale options, and the 1031 exchange. We'll provide you with the pros and cons of each so you know which option may work for you.

Now, let's move forward and talk about exit strategies:

Exit Strategy, What's That?

An exit strategy is defined as a contingency plan that is put together by an investor. The purpose is to liquidate or sell an asset that belongs to them. This is a plan that must be outlined and executed properly.

As a property owner that is in the process of getting out of the real estate game, it's important to think of yourself as someone who is looking to get the best deal. In essence, you are pretty much doing something similar to what someone else is doing while selling their house. However, as a property owner it's slightly more complex.

Clearly, you need to have a buyer that will acquire your property. When this process happens, you want to give them a run through of the property itself. This includes how many tenants are occupying it, any history of repair and maintenance, how much money they'll be getting out of the property each month, and the expense that goes along with it.

An exit strategy shouldn't be something you rush into. This is something that will take time, effort, and preparation. Not to mention, it takes the right kind of buyer to help take the property off your hands so you can cash out and be on your merry way.

As for the exit strategies themselves, we'll be taking a look at four in total. As mentioned before, we'll be looking at the fix and flip, buy and hold, the wholesale strategy, and the 1031 exchange. Which one works best for you?

Let's find out starting with our first strategy:

The Fix-And-Flip Strategy

The 'fix-and-flip' strategy is defined as purchasing a property that's a fixer-upper. You put in the money that goes towards repairs and renovations. Once the repairs have been taken care of, then you have the option of selling it as a single-family home for someone who wants to live there permanently.

Or, you can also rent the place out to a tenant on a short-term or long-term agreement. Regardless, you can keep the property in your portfolio for as long as possible. There a couple of types of flipping strategies: the rehab flip and the wholesale flip.

One difference is that with the wholesale flip, you'll probably have to pay a fee so the wholesale can find a buyer. Remember, the wholesaler gets the difference on the purchase price. Therefore, the buyer must purchase it at a price that is higher than the original listing (sound familiar?)

What exactly are the pros and cons of this strategy? Let's take a look:

Pros of Fix-And-Flip

Quick profit: This is pretty self-explanatory. With flipping, you can sell the property in as little time as possible. Whether it's selling it outright or increasing the value when it comes time to finally sell after a few years, you'll get a good amount of money out of it.

You'll have some construction know-how: Whether you do the repairs or not, you'll understand the ins and outs of construction work. You'll understand what kind of building permits are needed, what may cause delays, and be able to spot out even larger problems such as structural issues, mold growth, and so much more.

You'll be aware of the local market: With this strategy, you'll have your finger on the pulse in terms of the local market. You'll be aware of what's being bought and sold. You'll also get a good idea of what buyers are looking for. Especially those who are in search of a rental property that someone wants to invest in.

You'll increase your network: You'll have more people in your network than you know what to do with. This network includes contractors, building inspectors, insurance brokers, real estate agents, attorneys, and more.

Cons of a Fix-And-Flip

You may face potential losses: Losing money is the last thing you want to do. And flips can become flops. What could cause this to happen? You could be looking at expenses that pop out of nowhere. Property taxes could increase between the time you fix up the place and when you are in the process of selling it. Lastly, capital gains taxes could also eat up some of that money you've earned from selling a property.

Holding means less money: The longer you hold onto a property, the less money you'll stand to make. And that could also mean continuing to pay on the mortgage, taxes, and insurance until there is a buyer. Let's not forget the other expenses such as repair and maintenance.

Stress: Yes, stressful things can happen. There can be delays in the repair, no one biting on your offer, and so on. It takes patience when these things happen. So relax and come to the conclusion that a deal will be made at some point in the future.

The Buy-and-Hold Strategy

The buy-and-hold strategy is basically buying a property and holding it for the long-term. However, there are investors who are selective of what kind of property they want to hold onto and why. The goal of this strategy is long-term returns.

Your exit strategy would be to buy a property and hang onto it for as long as possible. Then, you find the right buyer who will use the property for whatever they see as fit. The longer you hold, the better your return on investment will be.

This strategy will work on properties that only have an upside in terms of value. So it would make logical sense for someone to purchase a fixer-upper, repair it, and generate income via rent. Over time, that property will increase in value.

When there is enough value to cash out and call it a career, that's when you begin to make your exit if you so choose. Other rental investors can just take it off your hands with little to no worry about repairing it (since you've done the inspections yourself).

Let's look at the pros and cons of the buy-and-hold strategy:

Pros of Buy-and-Hold

A proven strategy that works: Needless to say, it's a proven strategy that has worked to the advantage of many real estate investors. You'll know exactly when to get in and when to get out. It's kind of like investing in stocks. But you can get a predictable return on investment depending on the kind of property that you purchase.

You can hang on for the long-term: You can buy the property and hold onto it for as long as you like. This also means that you'll also be able to receive income from it and get a nice return on investment from it. The more money you get from rental income and the eventual sale, the better.

You are taxed less if held for a long time: Unlike short-term investments, if you buy and hold on to an asset you'll be able to pay less taxes on it. Yes, taxes are a necessary evil. But long-term assets that you hold onto will be viewed as more favorable. So the longer you hold on to a property, the better.

Cons of Buy-and-Hold

Markets changes: The market changes from time to time. It can go in a positive direction and it can go in a negative one. And when the market changes, so does the value. You cannot really predict the market. And for this reason, you won't know for sure about the overall value until it comes time to appraise it and perhaps sell it.

It may take awhile to get a good ROI: Let's face it, depending on your target ROI it may take time to get there. But that's where the 'hold' in buy and hold comes into play. Eventually with time and allowing the property to increase in value, you will see a long-term ROI that will work in your favor.

Looking Into Wholesale

If you are thinking about selling your property but want to quickly find a buyer, then there's a good chance the wholesale route will be best. However, what we should tell you is that the wholesaling method here is different from what we've outlined in chapter 6. Also, this shouldn't be confused with the wholesale flip method that we just discussed briefly early on.

This kind of wholesaling is coming from the seller's perspective. You'll need to find a buyer that is willing to acquire the property at a price that may be more than the listing price itself. So the price you set is usually below the average market value.

A wholesaler will usually purchase a home that is distressed and needs repair. Once the wholesaler gets the address and pertinent information, that's when they will contact the owner. From there, the wholesaler can get the owner to sell the property for a price that is below the market rate.

And of course, you know how it goes from there. What makes it different is that this time it's you that is the seller after you've rehabbed the place. Or, you can sell it at a price that is affordable even if the property is in good shape.

Wholesaling is a great way to build capital and experience over time. Yes, you may be sourcing the deal, you'll also need to find a buyer. Other than that, there's nothing else you can do.

But you want to make sure that the terms of the contract set forth by you, the wholesaler, and the buyer are honored. Also, you want to be upfront as the seller. So communication as always is key.

What also makes this different is that you are wholesaling the property before it even hits the market. Someone else will get wind of the property being for sale and then make an offer.

Now, here are the pros and cons should you take the wholesale route:

Pros of Wholesaling

You'll understand how real estate works: As a property investor, you may have a basic understanding of how real estate works. However, you'll have an even deeper knowledge knowing that you get to see the process from start to finish. You'll even learn some new terminology as you go.

More money in a short amount of time: This is a great strategy for those who want a large sum of money in the quickest time possible. That's because you will have the ability to have more properties under contract. The short amount of time is a few months tops. So you can make off like a bandit with a ton of cash in a single year if you so choose.

Little capital needed on your end: As far as capital is concerned, there is little of it needed. At this point, you as an investor will have enough cash to handle things on your end. All you need to do is assign a contractor to the buyer and that's that.

Cons of wholesaling

No buyers: Self-explanatory. No buyers, no deal.

Unpredictable income: With wholesaling, the income may be unpredictable at best. It may be more than you expect or less than that. Or worst yet, this won't give you a stable, predictable income. If and when this happens, set some money off to the side so you can be able to cover any additional expenses that may arise before the sale occurs.

The 1031 Exchange

This is the fourth and final exchange that we'll be covering. What is the 1031 exchange all about? And how will it work to your advantage?

A 1031 Exchange is an exchange of real property that is used for investment or business purposes. The number 1031 comes from the IRS code section 1031. The only properties that quality are those that are considered real properties.

In this strategy, a 'like-kind' exchange takes place. When this happens, capital gains taxes are deferred should you reinvest the proceeds to a new property that you want to invest in. One of the things that will get you in good graces with the IRS is that you don't acquire 'dealer status'.

One thing to clear up: 'like-kind' exchange doesn't mean a property for a property. It means that the new investment has to be a rental property. That's it.

This means with this new property that you have acquired, you'll need to hold on it for at least two years or longer. After that, there is no limit to how often you can do a 1031 exchange. You can sell the property and reinvest in like-kind properties while being able to build your portfolio over time and never pay capital gains taxes.

Now, here are the pros and cons of the 1031 exchange:

Pros of the 1031 Exchange

Allows you to invest in a portfolio: You'll have the opportunity to build a portfolio of properties if you want to. So this kind of exit strategy isn't for those who want to get out of the game completely. But you will come out with a great deal most of the time.

You can reset depreciation: If you want to write off any depreciation of the asset, then you are more than welcome to do so. And for this reason, you can also be able to reduce your income taxes that you pay.

Easy to trade up: It's possible for you to trade up your current properties for something with a little more value. You can exchange your property and get something that will give you more income in return. Plus, you do not pay taxes unless you actually sell the property itself.

Cons of the 1031 Exchange

Timeline is strict: There is a timeline requirement of 45 days. This will allow you the time to look for the property that you'll want to buy. After you have found the property, you will have 180 days to close the deal. That's a timeframe that is short from the get go, so you need to act fast.

Like-kind properties are hard to find: Identifying like-kind properties can be tough. On top of that, you'll also need to find separate properties that you'll want to buy so the exchange happens. So you'll have to field through the subpar properties that may not fit your investment goals.

Choosing The Best Exit Strategy For You

The best exit strategy for you will depend on your personal needs and preferences. If you want to build your portfolio from the ground up with excellent rental properties, the 1031 exchange is where you'll fare best. Most of the time, you may choose the buy and hold strategy as your default.

You can buy a property, hang onto it for years, and sell it when the conditions seem right. Or you can be quick about it and purchase a fixer upper, repair it, and flip it for a profit. Either way, it all depends on your financial goals.

Please note that selling the property isn't always the only exit strategy to depend on. You can exchange 'like-kind' properties and trade up.

Final Thoughts

Having a well-structured exit strategy will be key. Especially if you are either getting out of the real estate business or if you want to build your portfolio. Using one of the four strategies listed above, you will be able to choose one that will allow you the best benefits possible.

One strategy may work for you and another may not be your favorite. Find one that you are comfortable with. And make sure it is in alignment with your financial goals.

Conclusion

There you have it. You are now armed with plenty of information on how to build a rental property empire. Everything you have learned must be applied in order to achieve success as a rental property investor.

One thing that we encourage you to do is use this book as a reference. If you happen to be stuck with something, there's always a chapter to refer to. For example, if you are having a hard time with the financing side of rental properties, go to chapter 8.

If you don't remember one of the formulas for calculating the cap rate, chapter 7 has all the necessary formulas you need. All the information is in your hands and very simple to apply. So keep this book handy just in case you need it for any information or if you're trying to figure out what you need to do next.

We may have said it once, twice, or many times before. Investing in rental properties is fun, but it will take work to get where you need to be. And it will take a team of trusted people that you can rely on to help you find the right property to invest in, someone to manage it if needed, and the right kind of people to handle all of your finances, legal stuff, and so on.

At this point, you may have performed some of the actions steps that you needed to do. You may have got in contact with some real estate agents, built your network, and even scouted out a few properties for yourself. Or maybe you're a little farther along.

Even if you haven't started yet, you now have a roadmap that will help you build your rental property empire from start to finish. You can use every chapter as a milestone to get you from one stage to the next. Obviously, one of the first things you must do is accept the mindset that this will take work, but you have it within you to get the job done.

You will take the time to build a team as outlined in Chapter 3. Don't be afraid to put yourself out there and contact people who know their stuff about real estate and rental properties. It takes one call, email, instant message, and so on to open more doors and build a network.

And from there, you can be able to build your rental property empire from there. You'll have trusted advisors, extra eyes on the ground scouting your prospective properties, and people who will keep the property itself in ship shape no matter if it's vacant or occupied. These are people that you will be sticking with for the long haul, so be sure to give them some kind of value and they will do the same in return.

Remember, you must do your due diligence and your analysis before deciding on a rental property. The last thing you want to deal with is loss after loss. You don't want to sink a lot of money into a rental property that ends up being a money suck.

The path towards a prosperous career in rental property investing is no easy path. There will be potholes, roadblocks, and obstacles to navigate along the way. You may know what the destination will be, but how long it will take will depend on how you take on each task.

Your rental property empire may start in your local area or a hundred miles away. It all starts with finding that one rental property that will help you get started. From there, you can be able to add more properties to your portfolio. With a proven strategy like the BRRRR method as outlined in chapter 9, you might be able to build that portfolio faster than you think.

However, it's better to take it one step at a time rather than rush things. If you rush into it, you'll be missing a few crucial steps. Take your time and always ask for help from your team if you feel stuck on something.

Before you know it, you'll be acquiring properties left and right because you have the cash to do it. You can purchase one property, fix it up, rent it out, refinance, and repeat the process all over again. How many properties you want to own are all up to you.

This can take months or even years to finally reach your financial goals by way of investing in rental properties. So long as you set aside your emotions, be aware that it takes patience and work to get there, you are definitely in the right line of work to generate some awesome income.

Some say you might be crazy for doing this. Some will say that you'll lose your money before anything comes to fruition. But don't let the doubters and naysayers get you down.

There are many people who will want to invest in rental properties. But most of them might give up after a short period of time without ever performing a task like acquiring properties or networking. You may be one of the few that decides to stick it out, put in the work, and reap the rewards that so many have given up.

Now what?

Depending on where you are in your journey, it's important to move onto the next step. Do you have a team of people set up? Great...find a property that you want to invest in.

Do you have a list of people that you want to talk to about rental properties? Contact them during business hours or shoot them an email to plan a time to chat. You'll probably have a real estate agent even refer you to people in their network.

Are you considering the idea of refinancing your property and paying off the loan? Great. Go forth and do just that (but not before double checking with chapter 8 to see what to do.

This book might represent the next year or decade in your life. Use it to your advantage and you will have a prosperous future in your sights before you know it.

Resources

5 Popular Types of Rental Properties. (2021). Best Rent. http://www.bestrent.vn/5-popular-types-of-rental-properties/

5 Things You Need to Know About Rental Property Loans. (2021). The Balance Small Business. https://www.thebalancesmb.com/5-things-you-need-to-know-about-rental-property-loans-4772292

5 Tips On Preparing Your House For Rental. (2020, February 25). The Spotahome Blog. https://www.spotahome.com/blog/5-tips-on-preparing-your-house-for-rental/

7 Basic Parts to Include in Your Rental Lease. (2021). The Balance Small Business. https://www.thebalancesmb.com/the-5-most-basic-parts-of-a-lease-agreement-2124974

9 Ways to Make Money in Real Estate. (2021). The Balance Small Business. https://www.thebalancesmb.com/types-of-investment-properties-2124869

A Href=/Author/Peter-Gianoli Title=Plg_Content_Authorlist_Title_View_Author >Peter Gianoli16 Jun Budget changes impact both buyers and sellers, says REIV. Which Investment Property.
https://www.whichinvestmentproperty.com.au/blo g/13900-are-townhouses-a-good-investment

Abulatif, N. (2018, January 17). *Why Are Rental Properties Among the Best Passive Income Investments?* Investment Property Tips | Mashvisor Real Estate Blog.
https://www.mashvisor.com/blog/rental-properties-passive-income-investments/

Ainley, M. (2020, September 28). *Top 5 Mistakes When Using The BRRRR Strategy.* GC Realty Inc.
https://www.gcrealtyinc.com/blog/top-5-mistakes-when-using-the-brrrr-strategy

Albaum, M. (2019, September 19). *What is The BRRRR Strategy and Should You Do It?* RoofStock.
https://learn.roofstock.com/blog/brrrr-strategy

Andreevska, D. (2016, September 27). *How to Build and Maintain a Real Estate Investment Network.* Investment Property Tips | Mashvisor Real Estate Blog.
https://www.mashvisor.com/blog/real-estate-investment-network/

293

Andreevska, D. (2020, March 26). *The Complete Guide to Price to Rent Ratio in Real Estate Investing*. Investment Property Tips | Mashvisor Real Estate Blog. https://www.mashvisor.com/blog/price-to-rent-ratio-complete-guide/

Aragon, A. (2021). *What is Direct Mail Marketing? Strategies, Examples & More*. Sendoso. https://sendoso.com/direct-mail-marketing/

Backman, M. (2021, February 4). *The Pros and Cons of Townhouses*. Millionacres. https://www.fool.com/millionacres/real-estate-market/homebuying/townhouse-pros-and-cons/

Baker, H. (2019, March 30). *Investing in Multifamily Properties: The Pros and Cons*. Investment Property Tips | Mashvisor Real Estate Blog. https://www.mashvisor.com/blog/investing-in-multifamily-properties-pros-cons/

Baker, L. (2018, August 6). *Loren Baker*. REWW. https://reww.com/investment-property-loans

Bhakta, H. (2017, August 23). *The 5 Success Principles Of Rental Property Investment*. Gold Path Real Estate. https://goldpathrealestate.com/5-keys-considerations-successful-rental-property-investment/

Bilen, A. (2018, June 21). *4 Advantages of Purchasing an Investment Property.* RoofStock. https://learn.roofstock.com/blog/advantages-of-investment-properties

Borrowing to invest – the risks and benefits. (2019, May 23). Wealth & Lifestyle Pty Ltd. https://wealthandlifestyle.com.au/latest-articles/borrowing-to-invest-the-risks-and-benefits

BRRRR Strategy – Advantages And Disadvantages | TurnkeyPropertyPro.com. (2021). Turnkey Property Pros. https://turnkeypropertypro.com/property-investment-blog/turnkey-property-investment-what-are-the-disadvantages-and-advantages-of-the-brrrr-strategy-2/

Buy-and-hold investing is a strategy Warren Buffett swears by for long-term financial growth — here's what you need to know. (2020, October 15). Business Insider. https://www.businessinsider.com/personal-finance/what-is-buy-and-hold-investing-strategy?international=true&r=US&IR=T

By Harvey Raybould Managing Director, Creative Property Group. (2021). *Revealed: the mindset and success principles of a property investor.* Property Investor Today.

https://www.propertyinvestortoday.co.uk/breaking
-news/2020/7/revealed-the-mindset-and-success-
principles-of-a-successful-property-
investor?source=newsticker

Can tenant break lease days after signing contract?
(2006, September 28). Inman.
https://www.inman.com/2006/09/28/can-tenant-
break-lease-days-after-signing-contract/

Cohen, G. (2012, June 10). *Is Real Estate Investing
a Job or a Hobby?* JWB Real Estate Capital.
https://www.jwbrealestatecapital.com/is-real-
estate-investing-a-job-or-a-hobby/

Cohen, G. (2014, January 6). *Investing in Single
Family Homes: 4 Pros and Cons.* JWB Real Estate
Capital.
https://www.jwbrealestatecapital.com/investing-in-
single-family-homes-4-pros-and-cons/

Colley, A. (2021). *8 Issues with Buying Rental
Property and Becoming a Landlord.* Money
Crashers. https://www.moneycrashers.com/five-
issues-with-buying-rental-property-and-becoming-
a-landlord/

Cormack, F. (2019, December 18). *How to get a
home loan for your first investment property.* Lendi.

https://www.lendi.com.au/inspire/property/home-loan-first-investment-property/

Coverage for renting out your home | III. (2021). III.Org. https://www.iii.org/article/coverage-for-renting-out-your-home

Esajian, J. D. (2021, February 19). *Multifamily Investment Properties.* FortuneBuilders. https://www.fortunebuilders.com/multifamily-investment-property/

F. (2020a, February 10). *Landlords Duties: Repairs, Maintenance, and Notice to Tenants for Entry.* Findlaw. https://www.findlaw.com/realestate/landlord-tenant-law/landlords-duties-regarding-repairs-maintenance-and-to-provide.html

Fairless, J. (2018, December 5). *5 Ways to Make Real Estate Your Business Instead of a Hobby.* Joe Fairless. https://joefairless.com/5-ways-make-real-estate-business-instead-hobby/

Finance, C. (2021, March 2). *Fantastic 4: Assembling the Perfect Real Estate Investing Team.* CoreVest Finance. https://www.corevestfinance.com/real-estate-investing-team/

Finch, C. (2017, July 24). *Exit Strategy: How to Choose Yours.* StartupNation. https://startupnation.com/manage-your-business/choosing-exit-strategy/

Frankel, M. C. (2020, December 11). *Buying an Investment Property: 3 Ways to Make Your Offer Stand Out.* Millionacres. https://www.fool.com/millionacres/real-estate-investing/articles/buying-an-investment-property-3-ways-to-make-your-offer-stand-out/

G. (2020b, November 28). *12 Pros and Cons of Investing in a Multifamily Home.* Green Residential. https://www.greenresidential.com/12-pros-cons-investing-multifamily-home/

Goodwin, K. (2017a, November 8). *Why Is Real Estate Market Analysis So Important?* Property Metrics. https://propertymetrics.com/blog/why-is-real-estate-market-analysis-so-important/

Goodwin, K. (2017b, November 8). *Why Is Real Estate Market Analysis So Important?* Property Metrics. https://propertymetrics.com/blog/why-is-real-estate-market-analysis-so-important/

Gray, R. (2020, July 24). *07/05/15: Putting Together Your Real Estate Investment Team.* The Real Estate Guys Radio Show.

https://realestateguysradio.com/b070515-putting-together-your-real-estate-investment-team/

Greene, D. (2019, July 11). *7 Reasons Why Long Distance Investing Isn't As Risky As You Think.* Forbes. https://www.forbes.com/sites/davidgreene/2019/07/10/7-reasons-why-long-distance-investing-isnt-as-risky-as-you-think/?sh=7bf56813669e

H. (2019a, August 15). *How to Decide Which Exit Strategy for Real Estate Investments is Right for Your Business.* Homevestors Franchise. https://homevestorsfranchise.com/blog/nationwide/2019/08/how-to-decide-which-exit-strategy-for-real-estate-investments-is-right-for-your-business/

Hamed, E. (2018a, June 20). *6 Types of Loans for Investment Properties in Real Estate.* Investment Property Tips | Mashvisor Real Estate Blog. https://www.mashvisor.com/blog/6-types-loans-for-investment-properties/

Hamed, E. (2018b, September 13). *The Pros and Cons of Investing in a Fixer Upper.* Investment Property Tips | Mashvisor Real Estate Blog. https://www.mashvisor.com/blog/pros-cons-investing-fixer-upper/

Herriges, D. (2020, September 2). *What Vacancy Rates Tell You About a Housing Shortage (And What They Don't).* Strong Towns. https://www.strongtowns.org/journal/2020/8/30/what-vacancy-rates-tell-you-about-a-housing-shortage

How Much does it Cost to Hire a Property Manager? | Mynd Management. (2021). MYND Management. https://www.mynd.co/knowledge-center/cost-to-hire-a-property-manager

How To Perform A Rental Property Inspection | SmartMove. (2021). My Smart Move. https://www.mysmartmove.com/SmartMove/blog/how-perform-rental-property-inspection.page

Insider, P. (2019, January 9). *The Pros & Cons, Investing In Student Property.* Property Insider. http://www.propertyinsider.info/the-pros-cons-of-investing-in-student-property/

Investment Real Estate. (2021). Investopedia. https://www.investopedia.com/terms/i/investmentrealestate.asp

Jahnke, T. (2019, August 26). *What is Real Estate Cash Flow and How Do You Maximize It?* RoofStock. https://learn.roofstock.com/blog/real-estate-cash-flow

Jason, A. (2020, October 24). *How to Negate the Risks of the BRRRR Strategy*. BRRRR Investing. https://brrrrinvest.com/how-to-negate-the-risks-of-brrrr-strategy/

L. (2020c, August 27). *10 Tips for the Long-Distance Landlord.* LawDepot Blog. https://www.lawdepot.com/blog/10-tips-for-the-long-distance-landlord/

L. (2020d, October 19). *How To Hire The Right Property Manager.* Affordable Property Managment. https://www.apm7.com/how-to-hire-the-right-property-manager/

Larson, M. (2018, November 8). *Pros and Cons of Investing in Commercial Real Estate.* Www.Nolo.Com. https://www.nolo.com/legal-encyclopedia/pros-cons-investing-commercial-real-estate.html

Lease Agreement Vs. Rental Agreement | LegalNature. (2021). Legal Nature. https://www.legalnature.com/guides/lease-agreement-vs-rental-agreement

Liu, S. (2021). *12 ways to attract quality tenants | PropertyMe.* Propertyme. https://www.propertyme.com.au/blog/property-management/12-ways-to-attract-quality-tenants

M. (2019b, November 24). *Best Property Search Tools for Investors in 2020 - Mashvisor*. Medium. https://medium.com/mashvisor/best-property-search-tools-for-investors-in-2020-68209f9bb972

Manassero, B. (2018, December 19). *The Pros and Cons of Investing in Foreclosures*. Copyright (c)2004-2021 BiggerPockets, LLC. https://www.biggerpockets.com/member-blogs/8266/80929-the-pros-and-cons-of-investing-in-foreclosures

Manolas, K. (2020, October 14). *6 Types of Nightmare Tenants and How to Avoid Them*. Avail. https://www.avail.co/education/articles/6-types-of-nightmare-tenants-and-how-to-avoid-them

Mansur, N. (2017, December 8). *5 Risks Associated with Owning a Rental Property*. Investment Property Tips | Mashvisor Real Estate Blog. https://www.mashvisor.com/blog/risks-owning-rental-property-2/

Mattson, C. R. B. R. (2013, September 7). *Advantages and Disadvantages of Flipping Houses*. Coldwell Banker Rizzo Mattson, Realtors. https://www.rizzomattson.com/blog/posts/2013/09/07/advantages-and-disadvantages-of-flipping-houses/

Mburugu, C. (2020, September 21). *Single Family Homes: Advantages & Disadvantages*. Investment Property Tips | Mashvisor Real Estate Blog. https://www.mashvisor.com/blog/single-family-homes-advantages-disadvantages/

McDonnell, M. (2021). *1031 Exchanges Provide Exit Strategy for Business Owners*. 1031 Corp. https://www.1031corp.com/exchanging-thoughts-blog/bid/87004/1031-exchanges-provide-exit-strategy-for-business-owners

McLean, R. (2013, October 15). *How Positive Cash Flow Properties Can Make You Financially Free (Ep6)*. On Property. https://onproperty.com.au/positive-cash-flow-properties-can-make-financially-free/

Merrill, T. (2015, March 6). *Key Principles of Real Estate Investing*. FortuneBuilders. https://www.fortunebuilders.com/the-key-principles-of-real-estate-investing/

Merrill, T. (2020a, October 9). *Passive Income Real Estate Investing*. FortuneBuilders. https://www.fortunebuilders.com/passive-income-real-estate/

Merrill, T. (2020b, November 13). *The Pros and Cons Of Real Estate Wholesaling*. FortuneBuilders.

https://www.fortunebuilders.com/the-pros-and-cons-of-real-estate-wholesaling/

Miller, K. (2016, December 27). *10 Qualities of a Dream Tenant.* Rentec Direct. https://www.rentecdirect.com/blog/10-qualities-of-a-dream-tenant/

Miller, K. (2020, July 20). *The Lease Signing Process for Landlords and Tenants.* Rentec Direct. https://www.rentecdirect.com/blog/lease-signing-process/

Mo, F. (2018, January 1). *The Importance of Real Estate Investment Analysis Before Buying a Rental Property.* Investment Property Tips | Mashvisor Real Estate Blog. https://www.mashvisor.com/blog/importance-of-real-estate-investment-analysis/

Nadra, A. (2019, June 5). *8 Benefits of Owning a Rental Property.* Investment Property Tips | Mashvisor Real Estate Blog. https://www.mashvisor.com/blog/8-benefits-owning-a-rental-property/

Okoruwa, B. R. (2021a, February 19). *5 Questions to Ask Yourself If You're Considering DIY Property Maintenance.* Copyright (c)2004-2021 BiggerPockets, LLC.

https://www.biggerpockets.com/blog/2015-06-19-pros-cons-single-family-home-investing

Okoruwa, B. R. (2021b, February 19). *5 Questions to Ask Yourself If You're Considering DIY Property Maintenance.* Copyright (c)2004-2021 BiggerPockets, LLC. https://www.biggerpockets.com/blog/property-management-vs-self-management

Owen, E. (2020, June 26). *How Will Unemployment Affect the Housing Market?* The Urban Developer. https://theurbandeveloper.com/articles/what-does-the-latest-employment-data-mean-for-the-housing-market

Owning a Long Distance Rental Property. (2021). Copyright (c)2004-2021 BiggerPockets, LLC. https://www.biggerpockets.com/forums/52/topics/212186-owning-a-long-distance-rental-property

Passive Income. (2021). Investopedia. https://www.investopedia.com/terms/p/passiveincome.asp

Peake, H. (2019, August 6). *A Landlord's Guide to Handling Difficult People.* Rentec Direct. https://www.rentecdirect.com/blog/a-landlords-guide-to-handling-difficult-people/

Plessis, E. (2017, April 10). *Can I Afford to Buy Rental Property?* Copyright (c)2004-2021 BiggerPockets, LLC. https://www.biggerpockets.com/member-blogs/5417/50015-can-i-afford-to-buy-rental-property

Postorino, S. (2020, July 29). *Self-managing My Property.* Landlords Choice. https://www.landlordschoice.com.au/self-managing-my-property/

ProsperiGuide - Beware: Risk Is Everywhere. (2021). Prosper Guide. https://ovintiv.prosperiguide.com/investing/grow-your-money/risk-and-return/000342?survey=true

R. (2021, January 28). *Pros and Cons of Investing in Multi-Family Properties.* Trion Properties. https://trion-properties.com/education/articles/pros-and-cons-of-investing-in-multi-family-properties/

Real Estate Investment Analysis. (2019, January 29). Maverickinvestorgroup.Com. https://www.maverickinvestorgroup.com/resources/real-estate-investment-analysis

Rental Properties: Pros and Cons. (2021). Investopedia.

https://www.investopedia.com/articles/investing/0 51515/pros-cons-owning-rental-property.asp

Rental Property Inspection. (2020, November 30). Signature Home Inspection. https://www.signaturemore.com/rental-property-inspection/

Rozenberg, B. S. (2021, January 6). *Why Some People Will Never Succeed (& Others Always Will)*. Copyright (c)2004-2021 BiggerPockets, LLC. https://www.biggerpockets.com/blog/2015-04-25-success-principles-rental-property-owners

Rumora, B. E. (2021a, February 23). *8 Simple Steps to Close Real Estate Deals Like a Rockstar*. Copyright (c)2004-2021 BiggerPockets, LLC. https://www.biggerpockets.com/blog/2015-01-14-real-estate-business-not-hobby

Rumora, B. E. (2021b, February 23). *8 Simple Steps to Close Real Estate Deals Like a Rockstar*. Copyright (c)2004-2021 BiggerPockets, LLC. https://www.biggerpockets.com/blog/team-members-property-management

Santarelli, M. (2020a, June 5). *How to Self-Manage Your Properties*. Passive Real Estate Investing. https://www.passiverealestateinvesting.com/how-to-self-manage-your-properties/

Santarelli, M. (2020b, September 19). *Risks In Rental Property Investing - Norada Real Estate*. Norada Real Estate Investments. https://www.noradarealestate.com/blog/risks-in-rental-property-investing/

Student rental accommodations: The pros and the cons for landlords. (2021). Hawksby. https://www.hawksbys.net/news/2955/Student-rental-accommodation-the-pros-and-the-cons-for-landlords

T. (2019c, June 27). *How to make an offer on a house*. Trulia Guides. https://www.trulia.com/guides/how-to-make-an-offer-on-a-house/

Tak, C. (2019, October 17). *The Rental Application Process: What to Expect When Applying for an Apartment*. Apartment Living Tips - Apartment Tips from ApartmentGuide.Com. https://www.apartmentguide.com/blog/rental-application-process/

The Educated Landlord. (2021). *7 Ways To Increase Rental Property Cash Flow*. https://theeducatedlandlord.com/increase-rental-property-cash-flow/

Thinking About Buying a Foreclosure? Consider the Pros and Cons First. (2021). The Balance. https://www.thebalance.com/the-drawbacks-to-buying-foreclosures-1798184

Turner, K. (2018, February 6). *The definition of property investment.* Your Investment Property Mag. https://www.yourinvestmentpropertymag.com.au/news/the-definition-of-property-investment-246343.aspx

What do I need to know to self-manage my rental property? (2021). Ray White. https://nz.raywhite.com/blog/advice-and-tips/what-do-i-need-to-know-to-self-manage-my-rental-property/

What Is an Investment Property? (2021). Investopedia. https://www.investopedia.com/terms/i/investment-property.asp

What to Form an Exit Strategy. (2021). Investopedia. https://www.investopedia.com/terms/e/exitstrategy.asp

What to Include in a Rental Agreement [For Landlords] | SmartMove. (2021). My Smart Move.

https://www.mysmartmove.com/SmartMove/blog/
common-terms-include-in-rental-agreement.page

What's an MLS? (2021). NAR Realtor.
https://www.nar.realtor/nar-doj-
settlement/multiple-listing-service-mls-what-is-it

White, S. M. (2019, February 15). *What Happens if
a Tenant Breaks the Lease Early and Moves Out?*
RentPrep. https://rentprep.com/leasing-
questions/landlord-guide-what-happens-when-a-
tenant-breaks-their-lease/

WHY DO RENTAL PROPERTY OWNERS FAIL?
(2021). Rental Property Investing Rivera Maya.
https://rentalpropertyinvestingrivieramaya.com/wh
y-do-rental-property-owners-fail.html

*Why Does Property Location Matter in Real Estate
Investing?* (2020a, December 16). Vista
Residences.
https://www.vistaresidences.com.ph/blog/why-
does-property-location-matter-in-real-estate-
investing

*Why Does Property Location Matter in Real Estate
Investing?* (2020b, December 16). Vista
Residences.
https://www.vistaresidences.com.ph/blog/why-

does-property-location-matter-in-real-estate-investing

Wittwer, J. (2021). *Rental Property Cash Flow*. Vertex42.Com. https://www.vertex42.com/ExcelTemplates/rental-cash-flow-analysis.html

Woodruff, J. (2019, March 4). *The Advantages and Disadvantages of Debt and Equity Financing*. Small Business - Chron.Com. https://smallbusiness.chron.com/advantages-disadvantages-debt-equity-financing-55504.html

www.ingramcontent.com/pod-product-compliance
Lightning Source LLC
Chambersburg PA
CBHW030453210326
41597CB00013B/649